Facilitating Collaboration

Notes On Facilitation
For Experienced Collaborators

Brandon Klein & Dan Newman

Published by The Value Web

the value web

Designed and illustrated by Alfredo Carlo and Marcello Petruzzi
Photos by Alfredo Carlo
Fonts: Fedra Serif A, Replica, Adobe Garamond
Printing by Tipografia Altedo Srl

Ist Edition
Printed in Italy, May 2016
ISBN 978-0-692-68925-7

ISBN 978-0-692-68925-7
90000>

9 780692 689257

We shall not cease from exploration
And the end of all our exploring
Will be to arrive where we started
And know the place for the first time.

Four Quartets, T.S. Eliot

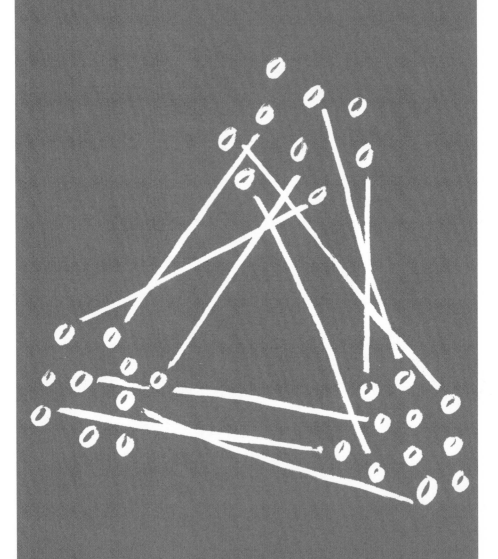

FACILITATING
COLLABORATION

CONTENTS

When Brandon proposed re-writing my book *From the Front of the Room: Notes on Facilitation for Experienced Practitioners*, adding his experiences to illustrate my reflections on method, my first reaction was, "This is insane!" Insane because a book is a book and Brandon wants to cut and paste my book to make another book I never intended. Insane because, though we are both rooted in the same facilitation culture, our experiences of facilitation couldn't be more different. And insane, above all, because I considered my book to be very personal – an idiosyncratic look at how I go about this work and not really amenable to generalization.

But then I challenged all three of my assumptions. First, cutting and pasting is actually a creative process; *c.f.*, musical mash-ups or Jonathan Safran Foer's *Tree of Codes*, for which he cut physical holes in a book he loved as a child to liberate a completely different story he found within. Second, the differences in our experience might add a new dimension to the work – this is, after all, work around making collaboration work; so let's see if it works. Third, my experience of facilitation might not be so idiosyncratic after all; perhaps I'm fooling myself into thinking that my experience is in any way unique. And finally, it is very difficult to say *No* to Brandon!

So reading Brandon's re-write, I see much that I recognize and much that I don't. As will you.

- Dan Newman

The following pages are an experiment in the truest sense of community. There have been many books written about different facilitation processes and the one I happened upon in the summer of 1996 was the MG Taylor DesignShop™ methodology. At the time, I, along with dozens and now thousands of facilitators and participants, discovered that you could put intelligent design and structure around collaboration. Several of us have now joined forces in building The Value Web, a Swiss non-profit, which employs our collective skills and varied experience to create impact for multinational organizations and charities. Dan Newman, a longtime colleague, wrote the original version of this book. I have partnered with him to co-author this new version to take our learnings to a larger audience and to improve decision-making through better facilitation. I am proud to be part of this. The practices that follow, along with each unique story, represent a real event that I have completed in 17 years of facilitating collaboration. In addition to the community that makes this possible, my editor Jonathan Walter made it legible. But let's be clear, it is only my wife Meredith who has made all this achievable.

- Brandon Klein

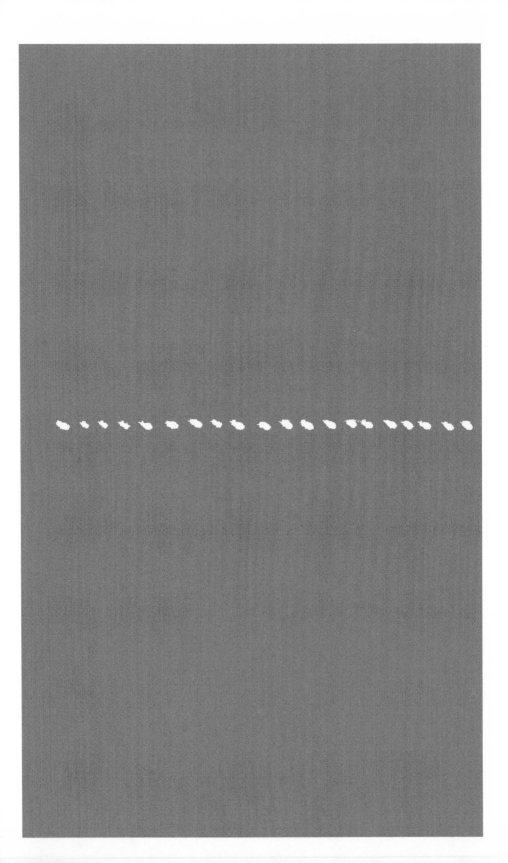

PREFACE

I quietly watch as participants, most of whom don't yet know me, shuffle into the converted space we have created for them. They expect a traditional off-site. They have no idea that the decisions and solutions that I will help guide them towards will affect every day of their working life from this day forward. I am determined to help them get more done than they ever thought possible.

With five minutes to go, I take my place at the front of an arc of chairs. I stare intently at my team around the room, letting them know it is time to begin. One starts the music. Others corral the participants towards their seats.

As they start to filter in, I try not to pre-judge those that sit at the front or the back. I try to engage 'friendly'; that's a made-up word, but facilitating collaboration needs to be new and if a new word comes out of my mouth, I embrace it in front of the gathering crowd.

As my team lowers the music, I fear the spotlight shining off my perspiration. In the friendly eyes of the audience, I suddenly see pairs of scissors chopping up the spirit and design of our collaboration into tiny pieces. I fear they will get up, walk out and return to business as usual, and death by a thousand PowerPoints.

"Welcome, my name is Brandon and I will be your facilitator for the next three days. To achieve more that we believe is possible, we must begin differently."

Music and my opening words are like the narrow neck of an hourglass. A great deal of preparatory work converges on that welcome, and an almost infinite range of possible outcomes radiates out from the same moment. As a facilitator, it is my job to ensure that we have assembled the right elements in the upper teardrop of the hourglass and then to provide just enough direction to the movement of the sand during the workshop itself and afterwards so that the lower teardrop fills up in the most satisfying way possible.

All the things I love about facilitating and all the things I fear about it rush through me in those first few minutes. First the love: I love working with a large facilitation team. I love not knowing what the solution is but knowing that there will be one. I love the music. I love learning the client's business, their private language, guessing who the good guys are and who the bad guys are, the secrets to their successes and failures. I love the environment. I love the design I've made and I can't wait to see how it unfolds. And although I'm usually shy, I love the prospect that I might be about to steer this gathering of amazing individuals towards something they previously thought impossible.

I love facilitating and I fear it.

What do I fear? I fear the surprise that the client sponsor will spring on me. I fear the small detail that is out of place (the big ones I can work around). I fear speaking too softly or too fast. I fear not being liked. I fear the superficial solution. I fear I have fallen in love with my design and will realize its failings too late. I fear the food will be delivered late or interrupt the momentary genius of a work round. I fear I'll mispronounce someone's name. I fear I might get fired.

This is when I sometimes spare a thought for the client sponsor. When I sold this event a few weeks earlier, I said it would dramatically reduce the risks inherent in the project at hand and dramatically accelerate their solutions. And though I know this to be true, I also know that the sponsor doesn't believe it. Handing control of such a large group of people to my team and me for three full days probably feels like one of the biggest risks this sponsor could take. I feign calm. I smile so that my sponsor can smile too and show the participants that they're in safe hands.

Where does my confidence come from? It comes from understanding the variables that will ensure the success of our event and knowing that these variables can be managed:

The Problem. We have invested several weeks understanding the problem to be solved or the solution to be designed. Most importantly, we have coached the sponsor team – the handful of leaders who visibly embody the need for the event and own its outcome – to understand where they are aligned or misaligned in understanding the problem.

The problem has been shared with the participants prior to the event, though there is not likely to be consensus or even much understanding of its nature.

The Solution. A solution to the problem *can* exist. No one sees it yet (or perhaps everyone sees a different solution) but we are sure that the problem is not insoluble. Even more importantly, the sponsors have convinced me that they do not have a pre-cooked solution that they will spring on the participants after creating the illusion that this was a truly collaborative process.

The Participants. We've invited a good cross-section of participants, representing conflicting points-of-view, cutting across the hierarchy, with sufficient knowledge of how things work and don't work. Everyone will contribute from beginning to end without interruption, particularly the sponsors.

The Inputs. All the information, analysis and other decision elements needed for the participants to do their work and take informed decisions have been assembled.

The Facilitation Team. We have the right mix of skills and characters to facilitate the client and sustain each other. We like each other and can have a laugh.

The Environment. We have sufficient space, light, fresh air, sustenance, access, furniture, equipment and flexibility to accommodate the type of work called for in each module.

Of course, I always have some doubts about one or more of these variables, but if I know what is in place and where the potential weaknesses lie, I can be confident and share that confidence with the sponsors and the other participants.

I greet them and I tell them the barest of facts:

"We begin differently right from the start. Everyone please stand up and sit down next to someone you have never met. Share why you are here and then our sponsors will walk us through the objectives and scope."

What I don't tell them is that we are going to do some remarkable things together.

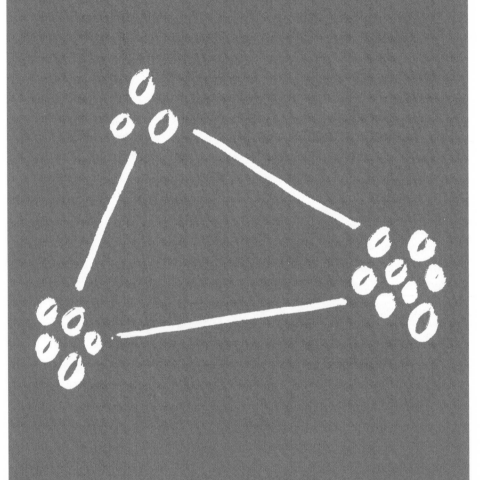

CHAPTER 1
FACILITATION, DESIGN, AND THE REST

This book is intended for experienced facilitators – those who know how to design an outstanding workshop and know how, alone or as part of a team, to deliver one. In a sense, this book will only be of value to you if, deep down, you already know everything that is written here.

This book is *not* about event design or building an agenda. There are many outstanding design methodologies, some of which I am familiar with and one of which, MGTaylor's DesignShop™ methodology, I have been trying to master since I was first introduced to it in 1996. I have experienced and used several others, including Open Space, LEAN, Theory U, World Café, Scrum/Agile and many derivations of Design Thinking approaches: from Target and IDEO to numerous derivations of Wicked & Empathy problem solving techniques from Stanford's Design School. I have met the fantastic people that have taken these and made their own amazing iterations. I am in no position to improve on them or replace them.

Rather, this book is about the facilitation experience – interacting with clients, participants, and colleagues[1] to create a brief moment of great possibility. I hope it is pertinent regardless of the design methodology you employ, if you employ one at all.

Many methodologies for conducting large meetings and workshops are based on codifying – making explicit and repeatable – the things

---

[1] Some terminology: Clients are the people – companies and individuals – who call for our services and, hopefully, pay our bills. Sponsors are the sub-set of participants, usually including the individual we refer to as our client, who co-design the event with us and take responsibility for its success. Participants are invited by sponsors to fill the seats and, with luck, find themselves changed by our work.

we do intuitively when we are at our best. Likewise, this book tries to decipher those techniques and ideas I employ and the observations I make while in the act of facilitating, based on my experience and intuition, and to make these explicit and repeatable. While most methodologies are built from models and tools, facilitation is created out of behaviors and techniques. The behaviors and techniques that I make use of as a facilitator are the subject of this book.

ESSENTIAL ELEMENTS FOR A SUCCESSFUL EVENT

Apart from facilitation and design, there are at least four other elements needed for a successful workshop or other collaborative event:

Convening
Getting the right people there.

Content
Assembling a single version of the truth – or multiple versions for the participants to sift through – with all the supporting data and analysis to make this truth understandable.

Ecosystem Management
Looking after all the moving parts – logistics, environment, facilitation team, knowledge objects – that add up to a seamless experience for participants. (We also call this Process Facilitation.)

Data and Social Content
Utilizing information about each individual participant, their interactions and networks with other participants and their own unique purpose and personal driving points that influence their work. This also includes the data and information that each participant contributes prior to and during the session. The wealth of content that each individual brings to a collaboration is essential.

Event sponsors tend to focus on facilitation and design while

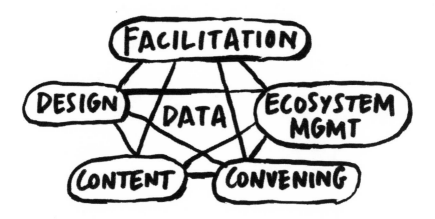

ignoring or taking for granted convening and ecosystem management. They often focus a great deal on content, but see it as somehow divorced from the bigger picture of the event. Either they focus exclusively on the content and trust the rest to just happen, or else they have vague ambitions (e.g., team building) which they believe can be realized in the absence of focused content.

In fact, all six of these elements are essential and all depend on each other. For example, convening involves not just identifying decision-makers and people affected by an event's outcomes, but also inviting people who bring a sense of personal purpose. They must bring content (human, paper-based, electronic, or other), which needs to make it to the right break-out teams at the right time. This in turn is an element of ecosystem management. The design process itself is the object of facilitation, while facilitation can only thrive when the ecosystem is appropriate.

This book attempts to take a holistic approach to building collaborative events – an approach that treats all six of these elements in relation to each other. The overwhelming focus, however, is on facilitation – how a facilitator behaves when shaping the work of a large, heterogeneous team of participants. The other elements are presented here insofar as they relate to facilitation.

Graphic Facilitation

An essential element of facilitation is *graphic facilitation* – the real-time translation of a group conversation into visuals combining words and images, all under the eyes of the participants. When I am in the front of the room helping shape a large-group discussion, I am almost always accompanied by a graphic facilitator – a scribe – who listens, judges, filters, and then draws. While the artifact which the scribe creates can provide a useful and colorful addition to a meeting report or Executive Summary, the real value of the scribe is as a designated listener. There, standing before all of us, a man or a woman with colored markers is listening on our behalf, focused on the conversation, thereby helping us to stay focused. And when participants *see* that they are being listened to, they tend to put more thought and care into what they say.

Scribing is a remarkable skill. It requires considerable presence and attention; yet it doesn't rely on mastery of the content. At a high-powered event several years ago, I attempted to scribe a discussion while hidden behind a wall; meanwhile my colleague – a remarkably talented young graphic facilitator – scribed the same discussion in view of the client. The highly technical topic (barriers to investment) was familiar to me but entirely new to her: plenty of jargon and references to obscure names and events. Yes, she has artistic talent and technical drafting skill that I utterly lack. Yet in this instance she chose not to use these tools. Rather than drawing, which she does so well, she limited herself to words and to a single black marker, working with one hand figuratively tied behind her back.

Her result was so thoroughly superior to mine that I have not stopped asking myself whether I even know how to listen. Of course, we can attribute most of her superior performance to years of practice, but I'm convinced that part of her success was due to her ignorance of the topic. By filtering out the jargon and the technicalities, she could better focus on the deeper messages and the underlying structure of their discussion. By reflecting back to the participants those messages and that structure – by helping them see behind and beyond their own words – she not only produced a wonderful record of the discussion, I believe that she contributed to the insights that emerged and thus to the discussion's ultimate success.

A book about facilitation should have a lot to say about graphic facilitation. This one doesn't. The simple reason is that what scribes do is, for me, magic. I know that there is considerable method and discipline to their work, but I am unable to describe their role or how they go about it. Scribes are the yang to my yin. For better or worse, this book is limited to the yin.

DATA & ARTIFICIAL INTELLIGENCE

The essential future element for facilitation will be artificial intelligence: computers will be able to autonomously look through seemingly arbitrary content, objectives, participant profiles, inputs and so on, and choose the best path for the group and facilitator. For example, many Gmail users already have the ability to let Google respond to their email. Google reads the incoming mail, then crafts three response options to choose from.

We are approaching a significant inflection point for collaboration and facilitation. For hundreds if not thousands of years, facilitators and collaborators have operated on gut feelings. Some models have been tested, some evidence or scientific experiments may have been used to improve outcomes. However, most facilitation and collaboration are based on personal experience, employing every one of the six essential elements of an event. Our experience and a few templates guide our work.

Fortunately, more and more research with larger data sets is being completed almost daily, showing what does and does not work in pairs of people, groups of people, large teams of friends and even entire organizations that operate in different styles under thousands of circumstances.

Data scientists are the geeks who drive the application of large amounts of information into actionable items – but they aren't typically found anywhere near a facilitated session. As artificial intelligence augments real-time insights, we need to respond quickly as these outputs could improve our collaborative and facilitation abilities a thousand fold.

Perhaps the simplest example of this change comes from the world of marketing. In the early days, marketers would place an advertisement and then judge its success by the amount of sales it generated. Marketing has now become so sophisticated, that when you see an advert, that ad follows you around online and even offline right through to the point of sale.

Marketers can change the price in real time, according to the time of day you are shopping, the type of device you are using and your past purchase history. They can instantly modify the offering to maximize the chances of you buying it, because your habits and profiles have been compared to countless thousands of others who have taken the same digital or analog path towards a purchase. Your odds of successfully buying a product can be altered by a few percentage points, which can translate to hundreds of millions in profit for the selling company.

As the fields of both data scientists and artificial intelligence expand and become more accessible, their involvement during meetings and collaborative work sessions will become more and more integral. Future facilitators will need to embrace this output, especially during preparation, to differentiate themselves and elevate the quality and volume of work that their clients can achieve.

Although most of this new data capacity will focus around the content of the collaboration, it will not be long before artificial intelligence also dictates the event design and even the profile of the facilitator. While facilitators around the world are at the early stages of making this a reality, 'People Science' and artificial intelligence will soon become as central to the success of an event as graphic facilitation.

There will be books, perhaps even computer-generated books, in the near future about how this works and how you, the facilitator, can integrate it into your particular field of work. Data and AI are quickly becoming my design partner, my convening and content recommendation engine. Ways to integrate this, however, will have to wait for a future book.

For the record, I wholeheartedly believe that the learnings in this book will still apply, even as autonomous machines rule more and more of our lives.

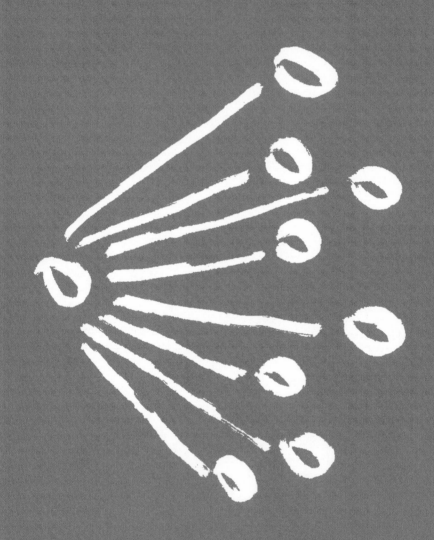

CHAPTER 2
THE FACILITATOR'S ROLE

SIX JOBS

What is my role as a facilitator? As the name suggests, I am there to make things easy for others. As a facilitator, I have six jobs:

Scoping
Understanding what the client wants. Scoping an event involves clarifying what outcomes the client is seeking, how these outcomes will be put to use to achieve broader objectives, what decisions have already been taken, and what topics will not be addressed. (see Chapter 3)

Working with Sponsors
Building a trusting relationship with the sponsors about content. Event sponsors will only trust an outside facilitator to shape critical work with a large team if he or she invests the time and care to understand the business issue at hand and the personal and political challenges faced by sponsors. (see Chapter 4)

Preparation
Assembling the elements – some tangible, most not – that need to be in place in order to deliver an event. Logistics and knowledge inputs account for the bulk of the tangible preparation. The intangibles consist of deep learning about the client's issues and the elements from which possible solutions will be constructed. (see Chapter 5) Of course, preparation includes agenda design, which

is addressed separately in the subsequent chapter.

Designing

The process of building an agenda. I *intentionally* choose event modules and order them to achieve specific intermediate outcomes and to create a narrative of the event. The focus is on the process of involving clients in the design process rather than on the design *per se*. (see Chapter 6)

Delivery

Guiding a group of participants through designed work towards a desired outcome. This is what people tend to think of when I say facilitation: standing in front of a room full of people, moderating discussion, directing work, telling stories, listening, and generally waving my arms about in the hope of orchestrating the work of a group assembled for a common purpose. (see Chapter 7)

Value Capture

Helping sponsors employ event outcomes to achieve desired objectives. The critical period immediately following a facilitated event is as crucial as the event itself to helping the client achieve valuable results. (see Chapter 8)

There is only a partial consecutiveness to these six jobs. Delivery probably follows scoping and preparation, while value capture grows in importance as an assignment proceeds. Some jobs, like scoping and working with sponsors, are present from the first client contact until the very end of the assignment. Design underlies all the others and is a constant throughout the facilitation process – we design an agenda, a sponsor meeting, an assignment, an interaction, an entire relationship. We design, we co-design, we re-design. While the other five jobs describe what we *do*, designing describes how we *think*.

No facilitator is equally strong in each of these areas, but failure in any single area spells a failed assignment. I occasionally have a large support crew at my disposal when I facilitate events. While most of them are usually available only during the event itself and a day or two either side, the opportunity to work with an experienced colleague on every aspect of an important assignment allows me to learn even more about each of these jobs.

FACILITATION SKILLS

More commonly, though, I have to play all these roles without much help. Luckily, the skills I need to succeed at all these jobs are more-or-less the same. When people ask me what skills to look for when choosing a candidate for facilitator training, I usually oversimplify and say, "Listening and storytelling." There are so many other facilitation skills, necessary or merely useful, from clear handwriting to memory for names, the ability to laugh at oneself, drawing, numeracy, modeling skills, good table manners.... Also, each facilitator has a wild card, a special skill that sets him or her apart from consultants or other facilitators and which helps establish the facilitator's leadership role during the event. Finally, there's another skill that can get in the way of good facilitation, but I'll save that for the end of the chapter.

Listening

Of course, everyone thinks that they're great listeners. They aren't. We aren't! Yet listening – not staring and nodding and pretending we're listening, but *really* listening – is the key to successful facilitation.

Approaches exist to improve listening skills, such as Active Listening, and these might prove useful for practice and self-assessment. I find, however, that techniques such as restating what a speaker has just said, in order to ensure understanding, can seem contrived and in certain circumstances, needlessly confrontational.

The most basic facilitation technique – visibly taking note of what is being said on a flip chart or other visible surface – is a powerful listening tool. When this is not feasible, taking notes on paper or mentally is always useful, whether or not the notes are ever consulted. This can be taken a step further by mentally cataloging the speaker's principal ideas and for each one formulating a question to deepen understanding of what is being said.

Note that graphic facilitators can help the participants listen, but they are rarely in my line of sight, so I require other tools to help me listen.

I often keep a notecard in hand and, just after a participant shares his or her views on some topic, I quickly jot down a follow-up question – not a 'gotcha' question to point out a flaw on facts or reasoning, but a focused request to dig deeper in an area that piqued my interest or that I didn't understand sufficiently. After all, if I want or need to know more about what a participant has said, some other participants probably do too.

You will always find me with a Scout Book[2] name tag. This is a mini 3x5 inch, 50-page notebook that acts perfectly as a name tag and note-taking surface. I wear it at every event and frequently, when I am not at events, you will still find me with it on my chest or in my pocket.

But the main prerequisite to effective listening is *caring*. If I don't really care what my client is talking about, I can concentrate as hard as I like but the messages just won't sink in. Luckily, this is rarely a problem since my moments of distraction are both very visible and off-putting, so I almost never manage to sell a project that I don't care about. The client picks up on my indifference at once and entrusts the assignment to a more caring competitor!

There is a way out of the caring dilemma: listening and caring reinforce each other. The more I learn about my client's problem, the more I care about it. My trick is to talk to as many people as possible. If the topic is too technical for me or if it falls too squarely into my zone of indifference, I can focus my attention on why different people in the same company see the same problem so differently. I quickly shift my attention from the realm of rational facts to the adjacent areas of personality, politics, anxiety, pride, conflict, achievement, and fear. This focus helps me listen better and as I do, I learn more and more – and even start caring – about the business issue that previously eluded me.

---

2   Learn more about Scout Books http://www.scoutbooks.com

A good test of whether or not I am listening effectively to my client is whether I remember what was said from one meeting to the next. A much better test is empathy. A consequence of good listening is that I start to take on the client's challenge as my own. More subtly, I reflect on the things I was told that seemed obvious or superficial or irrelevant and I start to see their significance. Empathy makes facilitation more interesting, both for the facilitator and for participants.

Apart from listening to them, helping participants understand that they are being listened to by us and by each other is fundamental to successful facilitation. Some ideas on how to do this can be found in Chapter 7.

Storytelling

What is so important about storytelling? Why should 40 people tasked with designing a customer relationship management system for 5,000 employees care about storytelling with clay molds? How will a knowledge of smashing and rolling techniques improve detailed customer performance software? How will knowing about Mendeleev and the creation of the periodic table of elements help a group of New York Daily News journalists create a novel online newspaper replacement? Because a well-told story starts out as someone else's curiosity and ends up as a talisman of one's own newly-acquired insight.

To find a solution requires seeing the problem in a new light, from a new vantage point. I tell stories early in the facilitation process to begin the process of conveying the participants as far from their problem as possible, and giving them a lens through which to view it from a distance. I always look for a story with some metaphorical connection to how I see the client's problem, though I rarely expect more than a minority of the participants to see the link. Usually, but not always, the story emerges from a broader metaphor or theme which I see underlying the overall problem the client faces. (I write more about themes and metaphors in Chapter 6.)

Sometimes, I tell a more personal story. Opening a large session for Google, planning their first foray into what is now Google for Work, I told the story of my experiences in baseball and tennis at high school.

I recounted how I was better at baseball and it was more fun, but I grew up in Singapore and England where there were almost no baseball players. On the other hand, I could play tennis all year and I had access to some of the best training around. I was stubborn and continued both for years. Switching from throwing a baseball to a tennis serve proved to be more and more of a problem and converting between them before each game became too time-consuming. My coaches encouraged me – first slowly then forcibly – to consider how I would shepherd my (rotator cuff) resources and energy to where they would have the most impact on my teammates... not to mention on the accuracy of my serves. As Google converted from a desktop paradigm to the new cloud, they had to let go of what everyone else was doing in their MS Word documents on their hard drives and fully embrace the future of every file online.

Several years later, at a large workshop to develop cost-saving strategies for patients by using big data to analyze remedies by body part, we told the story of eating a muffin. We described in detail the digestive process, from the taste, to the way the wheat and fruit were broken down by teeth and saliva, and how numerous body parts worked together to release the unneeded nutrients as a stool. We then spent a week with 80 data scientists, doctors, lawyers and more to find out exactly how to reduce the costs of treating diseases in each of those body parts that the muffin touched, almost down to the cellular level.

We used this simple story, of the body parts that are involved with digesting a muffin, as a metaphor for the diseases of each organ that we were tackling every step of the way. The muffin story 'took' and helped a disparate group of executives from actuaries to Zostavax treatment experts to develop a common language for reducing cost, even if they were previously unfamiliar with how the body processes a muffin.

A compelling story is a great way to launch a large event. If told with passion and a light heart, it can focus the attention of an entire room on a common theme, not to mention enhance the credibility of the storyteller – always a good idea when the facilitator is not known or not-yet-trusted.

I start even the smallest workshop with a story, though I'll try my best to keep it short. For a 12-person event on strategic alignment that happened to take place on the day of a new moon, I opened with a definition of the charming word *syzygy* (the alignment of three or more celestial objects) and the strengthening effect that this alignment has on the tides and on some animal behaviors.

What all these stories have in common is that they are not rehearsed; they are not even planned. I occasionally research and settle on a story in the days leading up to an event, but then I never use it. My opening story (which tends to be the biggest one I tell during an event) comes to me the morning I tell it, usually while I am showering.

There's no particular valor in not preparing a story in advance but I find that the right mixture of focus, adrenaline and stream of consciousness, one-idea-bouncing-off-another creativity almost always eludes me until the very morning my event begins. The story (true, of course) about high school baseball and tennis only occurred to me half an hour before the event began and I used it in favor of the weaker story I had prepared earlier. During one double event, the sponsor insisted I tell the same story a second time, despite my protests. Of course, it fell flat when told a second time and I have never told the same story twice to the same clients since then. However, I highly recommend re-using good stories with different clients. Employing a well-practiced story can drive home a point with a new client extremely effectively. Note: keep track of where you use your stories!

One of the purposes of telling stories and employing metaphor is to help participants find new language with which to address their issues. The design of a great event causes the participants to feel briefly lost and then provides the tools, ideas, and trust to allow them, individually or collectively, to find their way to a new-found (though, ephemeral) place of safety and confidence. A good story does the same, but all packed into the first few minutes of an event.

Telling a story successfully lends enormous power to the storyteller. By taking a skeptical or uncertain listener to a new place, a new vantage point, by way of a story, the storyteller has changed that listener profoundly. And if, from that new vantage point, the listener sees something new about his business or, better yet, himself, the storyteller will be trusted next time to lead the way on potentially more treacherous journeys.

To earn that trust, I try to tell a story in my opening that is initially of no obvious relevance. I want the participants to doubt me; I want to set their bullshit detectors beeping like mad. I have read a story about Ganesha, the God of removing obstacles. I have taught them about the hormones the body releases throughout a day, and which parts of their brains are reacting – especially the amygdala. I have retold my grandfather's World War II adventures as a pilot in a B-32 bomber. I have put an artificial intelligence app on giant screens and told the story of how computers are reacting to my voice to make decisions about the story's direction. I also rely heavily on my non-work experiences for source material, especially my time making a documentary film in a dozen African countries.

Without explanation, I take them as far from their problem as I can, so that the journey back is that much more novel and satisfying. When people feel lost and then find their own way 'home' or to safety or to whatever they are seeking, the path they have found takes on as great a meaning as their destination. As the playwright Edward Albee wrote, "Sometimes it's necessary to go a long distance out of the way in order to come back a short distance correctly".

Having earned their trust from the very beginning, I have the freedom either to choose stories that will require them to make great leaps of faith and imagination or only to take a tiny step away from their work to inspect it up-close and critique their thinking more honestly.

As an event proceeds, I will sometimes refer to my original story and sometimes introduce new stories, either to draw linkages between themes that have emerged at various moments in the event or to challenge some element of conventional wisdom. Here is an example of the latter:

In a session for a large multinational which had recently acquired 14 new companies, the session's purpose was to build personal, local, statewide, regional and domestic plans. The participants talked about iterating thousands of options together, fully acknowledging they might have to stop or even completely rebuild what they had so diligently built before they were acquired. The participants repeatedly spoke of the trade-off between quality and cost; they took for granted that in an era of tight budgets, quality and uniqueness of local solutions would have to suffer. While I have no way of knowing whether they are right or wrong (and had I posed as an expert on such matters I would have damaged my credibility as a neutral facilitator), I was able to tell the story of Saturday mornings with my kids who invented 'True Coloring Window Brunch'.

After a week of early mornings, my wife sleeps in on Saturdays and I try to take charge of the kids. However, I always struggle with what to do. Cartoons are an amazingly time-consuming (if somewhat evil-parenting) trick of which my wife doesn't approve. So one Saturday, I stumbled upon just asking the kids to draw what they wanted to do. Their first 'iteration' (I make fun of myself to the audience that I am one of those dads that uses these words with his kids. I happily admit I'm a Wall Street consultant recovering from years inside a Big Five firm), their first draft was okay, but it wasn't much of an activity. The next version started to get interesting and I began sweating because I'd promised them that we'd do whatever they drew. A mad thought crept into my mind – what would happen when my three-year old figured out how to draw himself flying? What little boy doesn't like helicopters and planes? I used the power of iteration and quality and anything else I could think of, plus his two older sisters, to draw another picture of how we could all fly together. The next three pictures got better and better and before long we were driving to 'SkyZone' – a trampoline park where you could get launched into foam pits. Amid the putrid smell of sweaty plastic, the kids all got to fly that day. Not only did they draw amazing things, but they re-invented what it means for everyone to be successful, perhaps redefining flying altogether.

By starting my story in a relatively far-away time and place (my kitchen counter) I intentionally interrupted the participants' train of thought, based as it was on unquestioned assumptions. The story took them out of their immediate challenge and gave them a new, higher challenge: how to improve each person's job at 14 distinct companies as a way to free up resources and define how they could all 'fly'.

This was a very small story and made only a marginal contribution to the flow of the discussion and the eventual outcome. Frequent use of small stories – whose pertinence is obvious – can help raise the level of discussion above the routine. Indeed, after my ambitious opening story, I tend to keep to business themes and hold back on the metaphor unless I am introducing a major shift in thinking, activity, energy, or tone.

The Special Skill

Beyond these two key skills – listening and storytelling – every great facilitator has another skill or attribute that makes him or her unique. I have an American colleague whose special skill is moral authority. He speaks and acts as if he is channeling God and the participants are in awe of him. A French colleague's secret is his charisma. He overflows charm and good humor and his participants want so much to like him, and be liked by him, that they give him great latitude in his facilitation. A Taiwanese colleague benefits from a phenomenally analytical mind and the ability to express complex ideas with simplicity and conviction. (These skills can also be traps – providing the magic solution to whatever challenge the facilitation process presents, regardless of that solution's fitness for the participants and their challenges.)

My own special skills are persistence and experimentation. Never give up. I frequently find myself channeling Will Smith and his treadmill analogy: "The only thing distinctly different about me is that I am not afraid to die on a treadmill. I will not be outworked, period", said Smith (http://bkle.in/1QuvMCn). No sponsor team or group of participants can outlast me. If a group even suggests that they can keep at it longer than me, I kindly remind them that I have worked with Somali presidents, Sudanese warlords and four star generals and they very quickly back down.

Since persistence isn't a wild card, but a least common denominator, my wild card is that I can experiment and innovate during every facilitation without fail. I manage to carve out possibilities, from a tiny surprise like a bike ride on the beach, to a real time software test with 600 people, to entirely new facilitation models and approaches. About 80 percent of these fail, but because my insatiable desire to experiment is known and frequently empowers participants, I am able to continue.

Although I sometimes refer to these individual characteristics as facilitation style, I believe that they reflect the unique skills of the facilitator; skills that can be cultivated by identifying intrinsic strengths and building on them intentionally.

The Skill Worth Forgetting

I've saved for last the one skill that can get a good facilitator into trouble: problem-solving. Some people are great at looking at a complex problem and immediately seeing the solution. They are often impatient with how long it takes others to see what to them are obvious answers. But it is not their impatience that makes these people poor facilitators. It is simply the fact that they see the answer at all that disqualifies them. A good facilitator should be the last person in the room to see the answer. A good facilitator keeps all plausible options open far longer than anybody else and feels real surprise and gratitude when the group finally settles on the 'right' answer.

Although I rarely suffer from excessive insight, I am occasionally asked to facilitate a workshop about a topic that I have deep knowledge of. In my days as a consultant I was considered an expert on digital transformation. Alas, I once facilitated a two-day event to redefine the customer experience and digital footprint for hundreds of external-facing websites converted into one portal. As hard as I tried to keep my mouth shut, my deeply-held belief that I knew what path they should take undermined my effectiveness as a facilitator and the event achieved only a small fraction of its potential.

The Facilitator as Disruptor

These skills add up to *disruption*. Paradoxically, the facilitator makes things easier by getting in the way. The facilitator is the rock protruding from the stream, creating eddies, cross-currents, and rapids while at the same time offering a foothold to whomever wants to cross that stream.

Conversations have a natural flow; they start when catalyzed by a new idea and then they tend to decline in energy and focus as they proceed. They meander and only occasionally reach a useful destination on their own. The more people in the room, whether active in the conversation or merely witnessing it, the less likely it is, unassisted, to go anywhere. So our job is to forestall that entropy by constantly thinking about all the alternative directions – directions, not destinations – that the conversation could go and then, at what feels like the right moment, throw a barrier in its way. The barrier might be a story or a challenge or a metaphor; anything that disrupts the inertia that the conversation has accumulated. Then we observe whether our diversion has added energy or taken it away; whether it has helped the participants discover new meaning and new perspectives in their conversation or simply caused confusion. When we get it right, the disruptions we insert into the flow will help it move in a more constructive direction.

To be effective disruptors, we need to find a middle way between a conductor who, unlike us, has a musical score she needs to stick to, and an explorer, who is simply searching for what is out there. We don't have a score, but we do have an agenda; we don't follow a random walk, but we're not certain of the destination. So our job is to shape a conversation – moment to moment – with the greatest possible potential. Then it is for our participants to capitalize that potential.

CHAPTER 3
SCOPING

Understanding the objectives and outcomes of an upcoming event is far and away the most important element of planning that event.

First some clarity on terminology:

Understanding

Understanding connotes a lot more than listening and acknowledging. I usually plan for an involved facilitated process just to ensure I've understood the needed scope. I will work with the event sponsors at length and over as many meetings as feasible. This understanding will be documented and challenged and improved at every meeting, including during the event itself.

It usually starts with a few words in an email or a phone message: "Brandon, we need to get four divisions of the government solutions market and all key departments – marketing, operations, risk, credit, and the call centers – to jointly develop a credible go-to-market strategy for a new product. The government customers will be making a decision in five weeks and we're all over the place. Can you help us?"

By the end of our first meeting (assuming they give me enough time – at least three hours, say) I will understand much of the terminology. More importantly, the sponsors will understand how their individual priorities vary and the extent to which their own expectations are not yet aligned. I will also have an initial idea of the six or seven precise questions that the event is meant to answer and how these answers will be put to use in the period following the event. This is all documented and becomes the initial topic of discussion for every subsequent meeting.

Objectives

Objectives refer to the ultimate result that the work performed during our event will contribute to. These objectives usually add up to some overarching goal (market dominance, cost reduction, survival) which motivates the client's desire for change. An event on its own will rarely achieve the client's objectives and the link between the event and the eventual achievement of these objectives is often indirect. In fact, for an event of any importance, months or perhaps years will pass before the ultimate objective can be judged to have been achieved or not.

- Most complex events will have different layers of objectives. The go-to-market strategy event mentioned above had several identified objectives and at least one hidden one.
- Align the various divisions so that the changes each needed to adopt would be compatible with the changes adopted by the others.
- Establish a common view across the government divisions concerning the expected benefits from the new product.
- Develop a sense of shared purpose.
- Make an impression of efficiency and clarity to the real government client and lighten the burden of subsequent oversight.
- Hidden objective: Establish the credibility and authority of the new programs senior vice president who hoped (successfully, as it happened) to parlay triumph in this sensitive project into a more senior role in the organization.

Outcomes

Outcomes are the specific, tangible product of a workshop: the decisions, plans, guidelines, vision statements, job descriptions, timelines, communiqués, and product specifications the client develops and adopts during the course of the event. Desired outcomes can be agreed prior to the beginning of an event and used as a checklist once the event is over to determine (perhaps misleadingly) whether it was successful.

Three Examples of Objectives & Outcomes

1,000 people to rethink natural health foods
stocked on the aisles of a leading grocery chain

Objectives	Outcomes
· Improve and validate the proposed future state of natural health foods & nutritional supplements within a leading grocery chain · Map an adoption roadmap for the chosen model · Address high-priority bottlenecks	· Mandate for a healthcare committee and guidelines for store rollout and scheduling/ prioritization · Identification of systemic implications of major changes and response strategies · Core healthcare process re-design (including organization) · Needs for tools to support new health approach (focus on IT) · Documented implications for sales process and key account strategy · Analysis of necessary in-store signage changes · Ideas for improving customer experience based on existing standalone store · People implications of new health strategy (skills, deployment, etc.)

Three days with 30 doctors and 30 programmers to develop a long-term vision
for care management for chronically-ill patients

Objectives	Outcomes
· Define and articulate the values driving the care management of chronic conditions · Identify, prepare for, and influence the future of chronic care management over the next 25 years · Inspire and mentor future leaders in chronic care management	· High-level 2030 Vision statement, including medical, social, political/economic dimensions · Detailed 2015 Vision, including measurable targets · 3-5 year action agenda for health care providers (clinicians, researchers) · Articulated 'user stories' and challenges for all key stakeholders, including those not represented here · Detailed prototypes and wireframes for mobile-based care plans

Eight hours with 55 non-profits, philanthropists, technologists and legislators

Objectives	Outcomes
· Link the immediacy of the current crisis to medium-term thinking about the architecture of the aid relief system · Create a common language to enable policymakers and the private sector to work in harmony to respond to the crisis.	· Shared terms-of-art (different terms and approaches to the same thing) · Defined avenues of communication with clarity on in-bound and out-of-bound topics. · Simple communication protocols to explain areas of agreement and disagreement among these key stakeholders.

Note the use of verbs for Objectives and nouns for Outcomes.

Objectives tend to be described as verbs, outcomes as nouns.

Deliverables are the physical manifestation of the workshop outcomes: PowerPoint documents, websites, posters, what have you – the artifacts of an event.

Participants leave an event with the outcomes in their collective pocket (even if the deliverables will arrive a few days later). These outcomes, in turn, contribute to the achievement of objectives, but only if participants, sponsors, and others take them seriously in the subsequent weeks and months and give them adequate attention and resources.

So much for terminology.

Frequently the sponsors have only a vague idea what their objectives are. Perhaps a project is going badly and they simply want it fixed, or they want a new business unit strategy because, as we all know, it is much more fun to develop a new strategy than to implement the perfectly adequate one we already have. And, of course, the more numerous the sponsors, the less unanimity on objectives and outcomes.

So when I work with sponsors on defining objectives and outcomes, the first thing I ask about is what success might look like. Although I take notes for myself, I make a point not to write their ideas on the flip chart or whiteboard or whatever visible surface I have. It is too soon for them to fall in love with their own ideas. They first need to listen to each other – the needs and expectations of the individual sponsors need to be socialized and compared.

A colleague who focuses on sports management always begins her client meetings by asking each sponsor to quickly describe their concerns and share their ideas. I fear that the first sponsor to speak influences the others, so I favor a more structured Take-A-Panel[3] approach in which all sponsors write down their ideas and only then share them. (see box) My colleague's approach is spontaneous and informal, but I believe that the potential rewards of a seemingly more contrived process outweigh the possibility for group-think which her

---

3   See http://bkle.in/1oqvboe

Take-a-Panel

In pairs or, better still, individually, everyone has 20-30 minutes to build their best vision of what collective success would look like. Usually, we provide a script, bringing participants out to the future to look back on their success. Everyone thus develops his or her own ideas in parallel without being influenced by other participants. I often find that many participants don't know what they think about the question at hand until a Take-a-Panel assignment encourages them to spill some personal ink and express themselves. As Leonard Bernstein wrote, "I don't really possess my own feelings until I've shared them." The subsequent sharing gives everyone the opportunity – and equally important, the sensation – of being heard by their peers. Since people frequently suffer from an inability to listen until they have spoken, this structured sharing of individual visions can generate real dialogue.

Here is an example of a Take-a-Panel assignment I used for my example above of rethinking natural health foods in grocery store aisles:

Mod 1: Take-a-Panel

This is an individual assignment. It is 10 years from now and you are looking down from above (or perhaps up from below!) at the highest profit per square foot store, reflecting on how different things are now from the way they were 10 years ago when we met in London.

Using the colored pens, create your own vision of our work 10 years from now. Write your name at the top of your page and USE BLOCK LETTERS throughout. Address the following questions. Create graphics and words to present your 10 year-out vision in a "stand alone" form that anyone could view and understand. Remember: a picture is worth a thousand words!

- *In this age of scarce resources and ruthless pruning, how did you prioritize health as part of your offering? How does this vary in different parts of the world?*

- *Describe the social integration of implementing health into an otherwise food-focused store.*

- *What sort of people are deciding to shop for health at a grocery store? What motivates them and how have these motivations changed since you entered the field?*

- *How has the balance of emphasis on prevention, cure, and long-term care changed in the past 25 years? How has this shift affected healthcare storefronts? Patients? Society?*

- *Describe the most remarkable changes in retail grocery in the last 25 years. What have our principal successes been? Where have we failed to make progress?*

- *The retail community has grown and matured considerably in the last 10 years. Describe this community now and how it interacts across competitors in the marketplace. What has been gained in these 10 years? What have we lost? Consider all relevant competitors, not just grocery stores.*

- *Many of the grocery chains who entered the healthcare marketplace in the last 10 years are now recognized leaders. How were they mentored and brought into the field? How are they now introducing a new generation to this retail environment?*

You have 20 minutes to complete this assignment, after which you will be given further instructions.

approach might risk.

Of course, some events have obvious objectives: for example, to develop a timeline and owners for implementation. Even these 'easy' ones need to be developed before feeding them back as draft event objectives. I try to explore causes, consequences, motives, adjacencies, and the like. Why is this objective important? Why is it difficult to achieve? What prize awaits should they achieve this result? What price will they pay if they fail? What alternative strategies can they fall back on? Perhaps that simple objective ought to be paired with, "Simplify all corporate processes" or "improve morale and reduce employee turnover".

No matter how ambitious the event, I never want more than two or three objectives. More than that deprives the event of its own identity and the subsequent association of results with the processes used to achieve them. And when I facilitate long-term projects rather than short workshops – six months rather than three days – I would never want to take more than one objective on board.

As the objectives emerge and I build consensus among the sponsors concerning their importance – both to the sponsors themselves and to the participants whose time is being diverted to achieve them – I refer to my notes and tentatively propose a small number of concrete outcomes. These often correspond to the possible headings of the Executive Summary that will emerge at the end of the event and I will frequently ask the sponsors, individually and then sharing their ideas, to storyboard the final workshop report and develop this imagined table of contents. I know that these draft outcomes will change before and most likely during the event, but I need a starting point from which to design.

I can handle a larger number of distinct outcomes, though I would never want more than the total number of participants divided by six or seven. If I have 65 participants, I don't want more than, say, nine or ten outcomes. By the end of the workshop, the participants will be focused on creating those individual outcomes, probably working in small teams in parallel. I would want the option of having at least six or seven people per team, so that would place an upper limit on the number of outcomes I commit to. And since new objectives often surface during the event, I would probably want to shave one or two off during the planning phase to make room.

Having distinct outcomes and objectives provides a useful reality check that I ask the sponsors to consider every time we meet during the preparation of a workshop. Will the outcomes genuinely contribute to the achievement of their objectives? What outcomes are missing if the objectives are ever to be achieved? What other mechanisms exist (probably outside the scope of the workshop under discussion) to assure a reasonable chance of achieving the objectives? How and when will we assess whether the objectives have indeed been achieved?

Out-of-Scope

Professor Michael Porter describes strategy as making clear tradeoffs and choosing what *not* to do[4]. The same discipline is necessary when scoping a workshop. There is sometimes a tendency to poll the event sponsors and simply add up their individual objectives and consider the sum as their collective objectives for the event. It takes a ruthless facilitator to keep objectives and outcomes to a reasonable number. As important as their number is their mutual compatibility: the objectives need to be MECE (Mutually Exclusive and Collectively Exhaustive) in the achievement of some overall goal, and the outcomes need to make a direct and credible contribution to the achievement of these objectives.

To help keep focus during the planning and delivery phases of the event, I will often develop a list of issues that are explicitly out-of-scope. These issues include nice-to-haves (for example, a pet project of one of the sponsors) or must-haves that can be better developed in another setting (for example, an organization chart with named individuals). I ask the sponsors to declare what won't be discussed at the event opening and I hold the sponsors and the other participants to these boundaries throughout my facilitation.

Frequently the sponsors will not want some item discussed either because it has already been decided by the leadership or because they consider it too delicate or politically sensitive for such a large group

---

4   "What Is Strategy?" Michael Porter, *Harvard Business Review*, Nov-Dec 1996.

to tackle. In both cases, I insist that the sponsors explain openly what has already been decided or what will be decided by others, thus framing the issues that really are open to discussion and design by the workshop participants. In the case of highly political or sensitive topics, I will privately challenge the sponsors periodically during the event to test whether their level of trust in their colleagues has risen sufficiently to permit debate and even decision.

'Scope-creep' is not a weirdo with binoculars. Rather it is the almost universal habit of starting to solve a defined problem and then allowing the problem to shift or, more frequently, to grow out of control until it is no longer solvable with available resources. I believe that scope-creep is responsible for more failed consulting assignments than any other identifiable cause. Scope-creep is just as likely to happen in a facilitated workshop as in a consulting assignment, but it is not necessarily as damaging. The key is to be ever vigilant; identifying scope-creep as it is happening, bringing it to the attention of the sponsors, and laying out the consequences in terms of how it will undermine achieving not only the original objectives but also the new ones.

Clearly defining and communicating what is out-of-scope before and during a workshop is essential to its success. But this focus on circumscribing scope must not become dogmatic. Scope is in the hands of the sponsors and should be the topic of an ongoing dialogue.

About two-thirds of the way through a workshop, I tend to open up the question of scope to the entire participant group. I might launch a discussion with the question, "What is the work we need to achieve by the end of the day?" What this question really means is: given what we've learned about the problem at hand and what our solutions might look like, let's revisit the scope of this work.

By sharing this discussion around outcomes with the entire participant group, we also share responsibility for achieving them. I will publicly and even ostentatiously ask the sponsors to sign-off on this revised scope in front of all the participants. When employing the MGTaylor DesignShop™ methodology, this large-group discussion is known as a Synthesis Conversation and it serves many other purposes as well.

Key Questions

In addition to defining an event's scope in terms of objectives and outcomes, I frequently identify several questions that I hear the sponsors explicitly or implicitly asking me or, more likely, themselves. The more difficult these questions are, the more useful they will be for me to help drive discussion in a useful direction.

For example, I may hear an unstated fear of a leadership team about the quality of their people and I will capture it as a key question: "Do our people have the necessary skills to achieve this degree of change?" Such an honest doubt allows me to ask the companion question: "Does senior management have the credibility and experience to lead the staff on such a journey?"

I will show these questions to the sponsors while developing an event and then glance at them from time to time during the event itself when I want to remind myself of the potential undercurrents and deeper truths that need to be addressed if the more immediate and concrete outcomes are to be achieved.

Some examples of objectives, outcomes and key questions from events I have facilitated can be found at the end of this chapter.

Are They Good Enough?

Once I have a good first draft of objectives, outcomes and key questions, the sponsors and I challenge them for appropriateness and urgency. We ask each other: Is this why we're here? Will the participants give us the best of themselves to achieve these results? Will we make the difference we need to make?

I remind the sponsors that the objectives and outcomes will be revisited throughout the event but that we need to have an agreed starting point to allow us to design and prepare a first iteration of the agenda.

When we are happy with this first draft, I subject our work to two slightly more subtle tests:

1. *Are these results achievable?* I am not asking whether the sponsors believe we will achieve these results in the time available, though we might indeed want to rethink ambition and

investment. Rather, I am asking whether there might exist out there somewhere a platonic solution to the problem at hand. "Designing the World's Best Supply Chain" might not be realistic for this event, but it is theoretically achievable. "Establishing a framework for permanent peace in the Middle East" might simply be unachievable, regardless of the extent and nature of our efforts.

2. *Are we being railroaded?* I hope that the sponsors, individually and collectively, have some idea of what the solution might look like. That's to be expected and encouraged, so long as they are open about their views (and we need to design modules to ensure that openness). But if one or more of the sponsors has a secret agenda, a pre-cooked answer that they expect participants to arrive at and, if they don't, that will be imposed on them, then we are being railroaded.

When I am asked to facilitate an event that fails either of these tests, I will either work with the sponsors to refocus the event's scope, or else I will walk away from the assignment.

Some Examples of Objectives, Outcomes, and Key Questions

Three days creating one of the first Accountable Care Organizations in the USA

Objectives	Outcomes	Key Questions
· Create a sustainable health community in Tucson, AZ based on the Accountable Care Act · Define the organization's governance model, operating plan and roadmap so that all healthcare system capabilities can be enabled	· Governance model · Documented value proposition and gaps preventing its achievement · Communication plan for all organizations and patients · Unified high-level budget for all activities	· How to reconcile the changing nature of reimbursements? · How can we build mutual respect between the different organizations being forced to work together? · How to change while no technology mandates can be put in place?

Some Notes on This Event. This event occurred a few days after Senator Gabrielle Giffords was shot along with 19 others. Much of the design was changed to incorporate the somber environment we worked in. We did several scenarios from the patients' perspectives which culminated in doing skits, allowing the participants to exhale and finally getting down to creating the solutions that are still having city-wide impacts. Big questions surrounded sustainability of the new model, multiple partner organizations working together and community adoption.

Two days with 110 participants merging 14 companies and their go-to-market strategy

Objectives	Outcomes	Key Questions
· Agreement, alignment and buy-in among key stakeholders for business plans · To come together as one team celebrating past wins and future opportunities · Non-project team members (central/national office) to assume ownership of the issues · Define centers of excellence for future integrations and acquisitions	· A working, integrated, end-to-end business plan by state and region for the next 18 months · A clear map of timelines, dependencies and tactics with other ongoing initiatives for the next 3 years · Detailed benefits-capture plan, including quick wins · Roadshow presentation to other business units	· Which processes are local and which are national? · What tactics can be leveraged nationally? · How will best practices be shared? · What decisions does HQ have? · How will technology eventually be standardized across all acquisitions? · What are the individual performance targets? · How will the end customer be impacted?

Some Notes on This Event. Creating complete and concrete business plans for each acquisition plus full integration plans to reduce risk while improving quality was the number one challenge. Different ownership structures and teams that had never worked together compounded the issues. Using Monopoly as the theme highlighted very quickly all the variables and vantage points around which decisions could be made, thereby strengthening the overall output.

Two separate weeks with doctors, data scientists, lawyers and healthcare experts
to reduce medical costs by $500 million within individual body parts

Objectives	Outcomes	Key Questions
• Consolidate learnings from previous cost-reduction measures • Find $500m in medical cost savings by body part • Create actionable plans to implement cost savings	• Prioritized list of data-proven methods to reduce costs • Timing, owners, barriers, gaps, and next steps for all cost-saving measures • Full agreement on working across boundaries to tackle each body part as a whole, not by operational division	• Does each cost-reduction measure meet all medical and legal requirements? • Can initiatives be financed and still achieve the needed cost reduction? • What can we learn from past failures and successes? • How do we make sure we always put the patient first?

Some Notes on This Event. This event was technically challenging. It took three months to prepare the data for the session – which contained over 1 trillion data points. The lead sponsors of this event had facilitated countless workshops themselves. Luckily, the potential for conflict or second-guessing inherent in such cases was replaced with real mutual respect and deep collaboration. This collaborative spirit infected the event itself which was critical because data scientists, doctors, lawyers and others don't typically work together in a high pressure situation. During the second week, we implemented a real-time dashboard so that all teams could see how they were progressing towards targets by body part and the greater success of the second session was attributed to this element.

Activate 2,000 medical experts to determine their future
education, career paths and patient care

Objectives	Outcomes	Key Questions
• Engage 80% of experts in creating their ideal employer of preference • Start to build team identity • Create roadmaps for improved employee engagement and transformation	• Project deliverables for 12 key trend areas • Identified improvement areas in workflow and communications • Reduce employee turnover and make the company the number one employer in the market	• How do we encourage collaboration between medical experts when they spend most of their time in the field? • How do we utilize the same experts to implement the changes? • How do we get senior management to accept the recommendations when they are typically the ones to generate and decide on the answers?

Some Notes on This Event. Given the large number of participants that needed to be engaged, it was prohibitively expensive to bring them all together. Therefore we used a 20-person sponsor team and People Science to actively engage hundreds of experts. Each project deliverable had four teams of four that developed it virtually. This dramatically improved the output and techniques needed for implementation to be successful. In addition, 500 experts developed relationships with each other and were able to share best practices and develop a community of support across the country.

Create integrated pre-sales and post-sales
implementation success for two organizations

Objectives

- Define and clarify roles and responsibilities to respond to clients' RFPs
- Co-create the best response across multiple divisions with client involvement
- Earn respect from one another

Outcomes

- Clear understanding of roles and responsibilities
- Identified improvement areas in workflow and communications
- Team behavioral guidelines, including interactions with other offices
- Roadmap of product implementation and 'sun-setted' applications
- Detailed RFP response

Key Questions

- Do we trust each other in terms of
- competence
- honesty/transparency
- How do we alter the expectations of client/ provider roles?
- Can we do all this work before a contract is signed?

Some Notes on This Event. Co-creating a solution before a contract is signed or even a winner is announced is a large investment by the client before any income. It also opens up the sales team to scrutiny from the client that they might not have the necessary answers. Although the risks are high on each side, the spirit and collaboration of the two companies made the session a pleasure and multiple more sessions were initiated from the very first event.

CHAPTER 4
WORKING WITH SPONSORS

The best predictor of the success of a facilitated event or assignment is the committed involvement of a small group of credible sponsors. Is there an ideal sponsor team? If so, what would it look like?

An ideal sponsor team...

- *...consists of four to six people to allow it to be diverse but manageable*
  Occasionally, a client will suggest that no other sponsors are required. Sole sponsors are to be avoided at all costs. It has more than once resulted in successful mutinies and almost always leads to unambitious design and superficial results.
- *...includes the boss, the man or woman who gets the glory or the blame and who pays the bill, metaphorical and real, for the event*
  This ought to be obvious. Not only does *the boss* need to exude confidence in the design and execution of the event, he or she needs to understand how the event is constructed before committing to accept the event outcomes.
- *...should include an intelligent skeptic, someone who will challenge much of what I propose*
  There are bound to be skeptics among the participants and having one as a sponsor helps to anticipate where turbulence may lie. If the skeptic is also charismatic, co-opting him or her in event design and ownership will help to ensure buy-in to the event process among recalcitrant participants.
- *...commits time and attention*
  I require face time with sponsors. I need to understand their issues and concerns and they need to develop trust in me and my approach. The lead sponsor is effectively entrusting the

next few years of his or her career to me; without sufficient time to understand each other, the sponsor's anxieties will spread to the participants and the trust that lies at the heart of effective facilitation will be replaced by fear.

I am rarely presented with a sponsor team so I usually have to negotiate for one with my client, the buyer, the person I call the lead sponsor. Since the sorts of events and projects I am asked to facilitate usually address serious or urgent problems, the decision to involve a large number of people in a workshop or related process will involve quite a few decision-makers. My client, the lead sponsor, usually involves these people in the go/no-go decision, so keeping them involved as sponsors usually isn't very hard.

One of the most outstanding sponsor teams I have worked with consisted of executives of a financial organization. My client was the late CEO of American Express, Ed Gilligan. The sponsors included a variety of leaders from around the organization. There were three, three-day events over the course of a year with 40 leaders. American Express knew it had to adapt to the changing marketplace. Just as they had converted from travellers checks to credit cards, the mobile revolution was just getting started. But the problem was that their tens of thousands of employees were not adapting to the new reality. In addition to practical organizational and operational changes that his people could understand and act on with confidence and enthusiasm, he realized that the team needed to change their mindset, and that is what we focused on for the three sessions.

What a pleasure it was to work with this team! Each of them relied on the success of the session to achieve his or her own goals. We used the book *Growth Mindset* by Carol Dweck as the basis for each iteration and module. The sponsors all had experience with both growth and static mindsets. What started as a simple session quickly turned into everyone sharing rich experiences within the context of the culture of the organization. We developed a series of modules for the year-long engagement across several cities and continents.

Another outstanding sponsor team stayed together for more than a dozen events over four years. The lead sponsor, the chief growth officer for a large healthcare technology and services company, was himself an experienced facilitator. He understood our approach and respected our choices, even when he would have done things differently. A second sponsor, the head of strategy and marketing, had an ability to explain our design and facilitation suggestions to the other sponsors with much greater clarity than I ever could have. The sponsor team always seemed open to new ideas and their own proposals were often in perfect harmony with the underlying design principles that clients frequently don't care to know about.

Difficult Sponsors

I've also had to work with some very difficult sponsors. One client was charged with developing a detailed plan to move one of the largest data centers in the country from Kansas to Minnesota. Just developing a plan and budget took 40 people three days, in addition to all the research beforehand. Do you load all the servers onto a truck and drive them to the new center? Do you transfer and sell? Do you just maintain backups? In essence it was an extremely complex and risky scoping exercise. At our first sponsor meeting, in an airless meeting room in Kansas City, I was introduced to the sponsor team, a group of seven client executives plus two consultants. As we made our introductions, one sponsor, rather than introducing himself and shaking my hand, looked at me from across the cluttered conference table, paused, and asked, "What makes you think you can move this data center any better than we can?" He knew full well that the CEO had put me in charge because other data center issues weren't always resolved seamlessly and there were literally tens of millions of dollars at stake.

"Luckily, I don't have to move it," I replied. "That's your job. I'm just here to help align your team around how to go about it."

At this, he and another sponsor left the room, though this did little to improve matters, as many of the others were equally hostile.

I tried to keep my cool throughout the design and preparation phase, with light-touch group exercises to try to keep their hackles down and setting up individual meetings with each sponsor so that the hostile ones could express themselves without having to play to their colleagues. I relied heavily on the *People Science Relationship Makers*

Handbook[5] to achieve this.

When it came to the event, this sponsor and his ally tried to engineer the team lists so as to be together in every sub-group; but with support from the two consultants, we managed to isolate them from the more delicate discussions. (See the Edward Teller problem on page 130.) Ironically, we held the session in the empty part of the data center!

The work proceeded steadily but more mechanically than I would have liked. This was a very technical event and my understanding of the content was sufficiently weak that I had difficulty judging the pace of our progress. Engaged sponsors normally keep me attuned to our rate of progress and flag problems to me before they become serious. Not this team, though. Only the lead sponsor, one project manager, and the two consultants displayed a sense of ownership over the event and its outcomes. The others were content to hide behind narrow tasks and rejected any responsibility for the event as a whole. Another big issue was that many of the participants had designed and maintained the current data center and they were nearing retirement.

By mid-morning on our third and final day, I was starting to get the sense that our progress was too slow and that we would fail to produce our agreed outcomes by the end of the day.

I pulled the sponsors out of their teams and brought them to a corner where I had set up chairs and re-written on the walls the outcomes we had agreed during the event preparation and re-confirmed each evening of the event itself.

I asked, "As I believe you all know, we have a lot of work without much time left. Let's come up with a new plan to achieve our objectives."

We discussed it and they felt that we could conceivably achieve three of the five agreed outcomes by the end of the day.

"Good, then let's tell the participants and inform the executive admins to reschedule flights for tomorrow", I said. The event was in

---

5   See https://peoplescience.info/icebreakers to access the People Science Relationship Makers

Kansas City, without enough direct flights to work past 5pm when we had originally decided to end, and I was basically threatening to sequester the participants until they delivered what was expected. "Anyone can't make arrangements to stay an extra day?"

My impertinence left the lead sponsor to choose between two options. Either he could overrule me, sacrifice the results of his event, and succumb to the blocking tactics of his obstreperous colleagues, or else he could back me up and blame me for the inconvenience. (A good facilitator always needs to be ready to accept the blame for anything – even the weather!)

Thankfully it was 'bring your kids to work day' and the CEO brought his daughter who joined forces with one of our graphic facilitators and stole the show. His leadership in getting the job done right inspired the more junior participants who then forced the 'old guys' to come up with the final solution.

We kept over half the participant group back until late that night. With the help of a large last-minute pizza order, they completed the work in half the time it would normally have taken. It was clear that our failure to achieve our objectives within the specified time was a direct result of a sub-group of sponsors working hard against achieving them. (The politics are too arcane to detail here.) Once they knew that they would be held accountable – held hostage even! – they had little trouble in delivering what was expected.

While this event fell well short of the quality of results we usually aim for, this isn't always the case. Another challenging sponsor experience unfolded behind the scenes of what turned out to be one of the best events I have ever been a part of.

Our task was to develop a multi-year plan to increase the number of relationships and 'collaborations' of World Economic Forum members working together to 'improve the state of the world'. This was a tall task and in order to succeed, we knew a new approach was needed. Therefore, we focused not only on designing every participant's time, but delving deep into the data and expectations of each participant. We tracked relationships with network science, social media and more. Creating a customized experience for each member, we increased the number of collaborations, relationships and the overall impact.

At our first sponsor meeting, a phenomenally talented group of people from around the world gathered. Our focus was the Forum's community of Young Global Leaders ('YGLs' – amazing people under 40 years old – think Marissa Meyer, Tony Hawk, etc.). The problem was that for the previous 10 years, designers, facilitators and Forum leaders ranging from Oxford professors to Imams to Silicon Valley CEOs had been in charge. They questioned us about our approach, our credentials, and our ideas for the event. In place of collaboration, we faced an inquisition.

Having survived the initial ordeal, we slowly won their trust and managed to develop a genuinely constructive relationship with all the sponsors – all except for a couple of legacy leaders. They evidently felt that our collaborative process which, in this case focused on data and real-time feedback about the networks of participants, under-mined and changed the traditional approach. It subsequently emerged that the organizing committee only agreed to our approach because we would operate independently, with our own data, approaches and responses, and without impacting anyone except the YGL members.

Nevertheless, two days before the official Davos kick off in a hotel basement just outside the security zone, we put together an ambitious design for 100 participants. I asked the sponsors if, for the duration of the event, they would capture on paper and their phones every notable interaction they saw amongst the participants. The only way we could measurably improve the collaborations was if our team served as knowledge and relationship 'weavers' – in other words, connecting and facilitating knowledge-sharing and relationships in real time. If one break-out group only had three people, our team member would note down the people still working and track them until the eventual outcome – good or bad. This would allow us to understand what worked and what didn't. It would also ensure that our design and usage of data would have an impact and provide useful training material for the machine-learning algorithms to create better teams in the future.

We did all this work in real time using both analog adaptions and software-based decisions to move people and content around instantly.

Although most of the sponsors loved this, including a fantastic lead sponsor, we met strong resistance when several sponsors and key members flat-out refused to participate. Not only were we asking participants to be open to the idea of data telling them what to do, whom to talk to and when; we were also asking team members, who had been delivering phenomenally successful events for years or even decades, to change their jobs during the event. Design and data were now equal partners for the first time.

Remarkably, almost everyone considered our open source approach (People Science) and the AI software applications we were using to 'tell' people what to do, to be more successful than a traditional design approach. It didn't hurt that one of the themes of Davos that year encompassed AI, self-driving cars and how many jobs humans will lose to computers in the next decade.

Despite the event's success, some of the sponsors who resisted the change were let go shortly after the event.

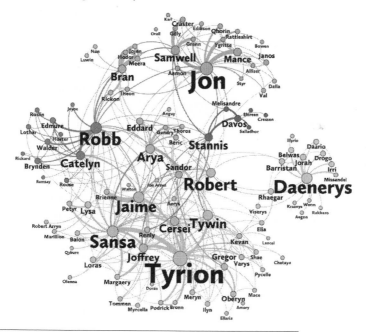

Network Maps/Models are a key element in improving collaboration and People Science. For example, this is a network analysis of the popular HBO series Game of Thrones. Printed with permission from Andrew Beveridge, courtesy of the Mathematical Association of America.

Client Infatuation

More often than not, though, I work with wonderful sponsor teams. For a sponsor to entrust us with a major event may mean putting the next few years of his or her career in our hands. To develop that kind of trust requires an unusual level of mutual understanding and respect. If this is lacking, the event probably won't happen. If it is present, then a strong sense of attachment can develop between sponsor and facilitator. The fact is, I really like most of my clients: as professionals, as friends. And they like me too (at least I am pretty sure!).

Sometimes too much. More than once, a client sponsor becomes infatuated with me. Nothing erotic or romantic, but a sort of puppy-love that derives from dependence and requited trust. One sponsor, the director of innovation for a Fortune 100 company for whom I have facilitated several events, parades me in front of his staff like a conquest – even touting simple ideas I have as genius (they are most definitely not). Once, in the afterglow of a tense, though ultimately successful session, she saw me consulting her number two. She came over to us and made a very unfortunate show of jealousy as if I was all hers and not to be 'shared' with the other sponsors. I have seen other facilitators with obsessed sponsors of their own and they are as uncomfortable as I am with these odd relationships.

I have read that a facilitator is a sort of transitional object for an organization, a security blanket or cuddly toy that helps them make the journey from innocence through maturity. I suppose that this problem of infatuation arises when the facilitator assumes that role for an individual sponsor. The sponsor can come to see the facilitator as an extension of his or her own power to effect change in a large group of people, a flesh-and-blood incarnation of a leader's natural narcissism.

In my case, I can identify one powerful characteristic shared by all the client sponsors who have come to be infatuated by me at some point in our professional relationship, though I can't be sure that this is anything more than a coincidence. All these sponsors, men and women, have great clarity of vision – they know *exactly* what they want their group to achieve – but they are bad communicators and their teams fail to see what their boss really wants. The sponsor 'sees' the solution right away and is then increasingly frustrated when his or her people fail to reach the same conclusions with sufficient speed and clarity. Although I may 'see' the sponsor's vision even later than the participants do, it is our work as facilitators that enables everyone to understand this vision, thereby making the sponsor *feel* listened to. The sponsor then sees us as the Aaron to their Moses, the interpreter empowering them to lead.

So, back to the ideal sponsor team. How about a lead sponsor who knows how and when to take decisions, and how and when to let others do so? Someone who has been with the company a long time in numerous roles, but hasn't been boss so long as to stop listening to the troops. How about sponsors who are comfortable in their skins and confident in their roles, who respect each other and who believe that there are still new things to learn. The ideal sponsors make themselves available all at the same time, and make their people available with facts and perspective because they want us to understand what it is they do. They never hide behind their boss or their staff and they *never* hide behind the facilitator. The ideal sponsors are fun and want their people to have fun. They respect our good ideas and challenge the weak ones. And they provide their own ideas that are usually better than ours.

I come across the ideal sponsor team more frequently than I deserve to. I currently work with one ideal sponsor team. The people on the team shift, though a hard core have remained constant for almost two years. The sponsors are the product of an outstanding corporate culture of collaboration, creativity, and respect and they see their role as renewing this culture through their example and their ambition for their company and colleagues. I would probably work for them for free, I like them so much. But they were for some time my best-paying client.

The Sponsor Team's Jobs

A facilitator has several jobs, and so does a sponsor team. In particular, I try to task them with six jobs:

- Developing and sharing an understanding of the event's purpose and scope.
- Co-designing the event with the facilitation team.
- Visibly owning the event and its outcomes throughout the event.
- Serving as the facilitator's eyes and ears during the event.
- Exemplifying collaborative behavior for the other participants.
- Translating the results into a form that the organization is able to digest.

Purpose and Scope

I referred to scoping in Chapter 3 and the importance of clarifying objectives and outcomes amongst the sponsors as well as between them and me. This scoping exercise is usually the focus of my first meeting with the event sponsors. Sometimes they know exactly what they want: "We need to translate our marketing strategy into a detailed work plan, with clear roles and responsibilities, deadlines, measurable indicators, and resource allocation." But this is very rare.

More commonly, the request amounts to something like, "We need the management teams of these seven business units to develop a common product development platform," or "We have to launch the process for developing our three-year strategy." In the former case, the scoping process might address questions such as: Why these seven? What benefits do you expect from this? What costs will you accept? How deep is the agreement amongst all of you that this is really necessary and desirable?[6]

But let's take the latter case – the significant increase in member collaborations for the World Economic Forum's Young Global Leaders. As I mentioned above, our first meeting was more of an inquisition than a collaborative scoping exercise, so the real work began in our second meeting. The fact that our meeting was held in a hotel ballroom helped enormously. You may have guessed this about me

---

6   I would never ask these questions *per se* as they invite superficial answers. Rather, I will create challenges for which meaningful answers to these questions will prove essential.

already, but I despise the 'innovation spaces' and 'war rooms' that architects of corporate environments imagine would be a collaborative space. Therefore, it was helpful that all of my guests (YGL sponsors), gathered daily in my space, the hotel ballroom which has become my home away from home. I welcomed them, offered them coffee, and immediately launched into a tour of the environment and the data sets we would be using, including a pointed, though brief, explanation of our method. I told stories about other clients' experiences. The environment was filled with two-meter tall whiteboards and as we spoke, a graphic facilitator standing behind us took large, illustrated notes of our discussion. I took a marker and wrote a list of meeting objectives on a whiteboard:

CONTEXT
OBJECTIVES
OUTCOMES } TODAY
PARTICIPANTS
INPUT
_____
LOGISTICS
AGENDA DESIGN
RESPONSIBILITIES
NEXT STEPS

I drew a line under Inputs and said that we needed to work through all nine steps to develop our event, but that we would only start to address the first five in today's work. I dashed any expectations they might have had of nailing down a detailed design. Drafting one before aligning around – and sleeping on – objectives and outcomes would have created endless confusion about means and ends down the road.

We touched on context very quickly; I knew that more would emerge in individual interviews. I asked: Why now? What happened to the last collaborations strategy? What do you do with more collaborations once they are set in motion? Do you know how other communities have developed activities that you're particularly impressed with? And so forth.

Then I wrote OBJECTIVES and OUTCOMES on a whiteboard and, much to their surprise, I gave them each a written assignment, directed them to a group of whiteboards (panels), and set them to work. I switched on a Gonzales track of solo jazz piano.

The Take-A-Panel exercise[7] took them out into the future, nine months after the end of the event we were planning, and asked them to look back and describe what results the event had achieved and how it had achieved them. There were 11 questions, probably more than could be answered in the 25 minutes I gave them for this work. The tone was positive but dispassionate, and slightly ambiguous, as if I wanted them to define the question itself rather than merely spit out an answer. For example: "Considerable resistance arose during the event to one particular collaboration. Which group of participants objected, what was their concern, and how was it addressed?"

I also asked them to draft the table of contents of the final report that emerged from the event, which is enormously helpful in teasing out the priorities and expectations of the individual sponsors and how they differ. Other questions concerned the preparation required for the event, the ultimate use of the event's outcomes, and provocations to tease out their unstated views on the Forum's mission (e.g., "How exactly will the results of the event design plus all the additional data insights impact the world outside the walls of the Forum?").

I turned down the music and then we watched and listened while each participant described his or her panel. I suppressed discussion, just letting each sponsor have a moment of undivided attention. I kept notes about what I heard and, in particular, about the divergences in their expectations and desires.

Only once everyone had finished, I launched a discussion on strong messages and areas of agreement and disagreement. They covered most of the issues in my notes without me having to say anything. They observed many other themes in each other's work that I, as a newcomer to this client, was of course oblivious to.

We walked back to where I had written OBJECTIVES and OUTCOMES

---

7   See p. 25

and started to list whatever came to mind. When their ideas revolved around verbs (align, agree, define, identify...) I put them under *OBJECTIVES*. When they stressed the nouns (responsibilities, follow-up, priorities, operating models, tracking...) I wrote them down under *OUTCOMES*.

We culled, we refined, we word-smithed, we rearranged, and after 20 minutes we had the first of what would become several drafts of our objectives and outcomes.

We then spoke about participants. There was a list of the 'usual suspects' who were involved in any strategic discussion in the community, and then people just started offering names, without rhyme or reason. I suggested focusing on three types of participant:

People Who Decide

By this, I meant people who would publicly take responsibility for the event's results and had the power of yea or nay when controversial decisions were to be taken. This group included the sponsors and perhaps an official from the board of advisors.

People Who Know

This much larger group included just about anybody who had an understanding of: how the community worked (members), how it *could* work (dreamers and crackpots), its constraints (lawyers, HR department, and other devils' advocates), and its potential (students, old timers, newcomers, neighbors).

People Who Implement

We needed to ensure that the lawyers, financiers and entrepreneurs (YGL members) who would have to take the results and turn them into action were part of each team from the very beginning.

We worked with the list of people to come up with all the data points required to maximize the chances of the right people meeting each other over the course of the event.

We spoke only briefly about inputs since I knew that the best inputs would emerge from individual interviews with sponsors and from the results of the survey and social media data we would be obtaining in the weeks leading up to the event.

What we most clearly did not discuss, as much as the sponsors wanted to, was design. I insisted that I simply didn't yet have enough elements to work up a design with them, but I promised that we would do so at our next meeting. And we organized the surveys and questions we needed from each participant in order to customize and maximize the experience for each person – perhaps the first ever example of this for a large conference.

This was a very good start and I felt that the event could indeed be a success.

This session was held several years ago. More recently, I found myself with a new client – a medium-sized, successful chain of urgent care clinics in the northeast. Looking back on the two sponsor meetings – different clients, different problems, different colleagues – I am struck by how essentially similar they were. In both cases, it took about three hours to learn enough to develop some empathy, to share some secrets, and to develop some common language.

This more recent meeting was held in a meeting room at a suburban office sprawl rather than in our environment, and this put me in a position of being their guest and playing by their rules. But we overcame this and found a *modus operandi* that served us well in the weeks that followed.

As a footnote, I should mention that when I hold a sponsor meeting at the client's offices, I try to make the space my own. In this recent case, I came early and removed the conference table so that we only had a circle of chairs. I also attached portable speakers to my Mac and played music during their Take-A-Panel assignment. Yes, for the first few minutes they thought I was insane, but they quickly grew accustomed to it and I'm sure that now, when they hold meetings in the same room, they are quietly disappointed that no one provides them with music while they work.

Is their thing even a thing?

One of the challenges of working with sponsors is deciding whether the issue they present actually exists. Myths abound and 'problems' take on a life of their own and it is our job to stand back and challenge our sponsors' assumptions.

I was asked to help design an event on the 'healthcare ecosystem'. We were struggling to find a coherent approach to determining whether new products and new integrations both internally and externally would represent a threat, an opportunity, or something else. Our discussion was superficial and aimless. We were behaving as if we were talking about something, but it *felt* as if we were talking about nothing at all. I try to listen to my feelings, so I entertained the idea that we *were* talking about nothing at all. "Is 'healthcare ecosystem' even a thing?", I asked myself.

So, as I often do when I feel it is time to keep the discussion moving in the hope that meaning will emerge from some unexpected place, I shifted our focus to a different level of recursion, to a level of greater detail. "Let's not talk about 'healthcare ecosystem'", I suggested, "Let's focus on individual elements of human care and then find if they share some 'emergent' quality."

In hindsight, it seems like an obvious approach, but at the time, the expression 'healthcare ecosystem' was so in vogue that we mistook it for a 'thing'. Only when we decided that healthcare ecosystem isn't a thing at all did we manage to make progress.

Shifting to a Different Level of Recursion

During a sponsor conversation – just as during any event – a facilitator is always listening for ways to move the discussion to a different level of recursion, to 'escape to a higher order'. Insights appear when we discover meaning somewhere *outside* the narrative we are facilitating.

During the same sponsor meeting about 'healthcare ecosystem', I was encouraging the sponsors to talk about the issues without really knowing where I would find an insight that would help with the design. I listened and listened and waited until they said something I could latch on to. And then someone did.

One of the sponsors said, "Yes, but what does it [healthcare ecosystem] mean for us people?" This didn't sound like a very interesting question, until I asked myself, "What if it *is* an interesting question after all? Could there be a higher order of meaning in that question that we could investigate?"

If there were meaning in that question, it probably lay in the word 'people'. So we unpacked the word to identify a series of dimensions against which to test the proposition that 'healthcare ecosystem' (as a *thing* or as a series of individual healthcare touchpoints) could have meaning for *people*. We expressed these dimensions in pairs: care delivery/chronic and complex conditions, payment products/financial support, data analytics/patient decision support... and furthermore, how healthcare compares to a town. We used streets/shops, houses/condos, commercial/government. We even tried stories above and below ground (e.g., parking ramps/sewer system), but that was one level of recursion too far!

These dimensions became the basis of our design and helped us shift the focus from the solutions systems themselves to the impact they might have on people and on the different dimensions of what it means to be a person. We were stuck talking about mere stuff until we managed to shift the conversation to a different level of recursion, a new font of insight. We call this 'escaping to a higher order' and it is investigated in Chapter 7.

Co-Design

I address the design process itself in the next chapter; here I will just touch on the *co-* prefix.

What does it mean to *co*-design a session with a sponsor team? How equal are the roles of the facilitator and the sponsors in designing the event?

In the best of circumstances, the sponsors and the facilitator work side-by-side to develop a design for the agenda and the participant experience. They start from a shared understanding of objectives and desired outcomes and craft the entire event. The ideal sponsor team is an equal partner in the design process. First, we create the design together. Then, in the weeks leading up to the event, they try out ideas on us with the same level of excitement and playfulness as we run ideas by them. Their ideas are certainly different from ours – they tend to be driven more by an appreciation of the content than by a desire to shape the experience – but they are certainly no less central to the design process nor are they less creative or insightful than our ideas.

In most cases, though, I find that co-design is limited to the (fundamental) work of agreeing objectives and outcomes and then to editing, improving on, revising, re-shaping, and fine-tuning a design that we, the facilitation team, have drafted in their absence. Very few sponsor teams want to be included in the detailed drafting.

Usually – when I'm working alone or, better, with one or two colleagues – the design emerges quickly and then is iterated several times before a draft ever makes it to the sponsors. The challenge is to not fall in love with one's own ideas. If there is to be genuine collaboration on the design, the fact that the sponsors did not participate in the development of early drafts can make for a stressful discussion.

The real problem here is that the sponsors may struggle to understand the design, not having been part of the process through which it evolved. Our insistence that event participants should include people who decide, people who know, and people who implement (see p. 47) is as valid for the design process as for the event itself. Therefore, in those cases when our initial drafts emerge without sponsor input, we can't simply share the design, we need to re-create the design process, the flow of ideas and inspiration, that went into its drafting. But describing an inspiration just isn't the same as having one.

So I find this process of co-design to be very fraught. At its best, it is as creative and satisfying as the event itself, just on a smaller scale. More commonly, though, it is a less-than ideal process, even when an outstanding design emerges from it.

We facilitators are sometimes accused of arrogance, of belonging to some secret society whose rituals we refuse to share with our clients. Alas, our approach to co-design frequently confirms the validity of this charge.

Thus, even when the sponsors are not fully plugged in to the design process, we need to help them feel that the design is theirs. Their critiques represent a useful preview of the queries – stated and unstated – that the participants will pose. This is not about fooling them into mistaking our work for theirs; it really must *become* theirs, usually through long discussion, revision, and, finally, through editing the assignments that translate the design into a detailed script of the event, about which more below.

What renders co-design essential to the sponsors' job is both the shared responsibility for shaping the best possible event and the necessity, during the event itself, for the sponsors to demonstrate trust in the process. If the sponsors feel alienated from the design process, they will be unable to demonstrate ownership of the event itself and its outcomes.

An important footnote: What co-design is NOT. 'Co' doesn't mean merging or removing your design method. It doesn't mean designing it to their method of large group discussions or rows of chairs and tables. It doesn't mean sharing your personal bias for *content*-based design decisions. You are the designer, not the content creator or opinion maker. Co is not jumping on the bandwagon of the most senior sponsor member. Co is not shortcutting because a traditional design or workshop or even PowerPoint is the simplest way. Co is not leaving a three-hour time block in the agenda and simply mentioning that a topic will be co-delivered or co-invented. Having taught hundreds of facilitators across various methods, one of the biggest problems facilitators face is when their principles and fundamental ideas become lost in an effort to collaboratively co-design.

Owning the Event

By 'owning' the event, I mean not just that sponsors accept responsibility for its results (or that they pay the bills!), but that they feel real ownership – that they feel possessive about its elements and pride about the choices that its design and execution represent.

But it isn't just the sponsors who own the event. There are three very visible owners: the sponsors, the facilitator, and the other participants.

The sponsors own the questions that the event is intended to answer and, to a large extent, the answers that emerge at the other end. They own the content and the scope.

The facilitator and the facilitation team own the process, the environment, the tools, and the tone of the event. Although the process of co-design helps build credibility for the process, the ultimate ownership of the process underpinning that design rests with them; sharing that ownership with sponsors or others undermines the trust – necessarily blind trust – that participants need to invest in the process.

What does that leave for the participants to own? Well, at the beginning of an event, the participants often feel like guests at their own party. They own neither the content nor the process; instead they find themselves caught up in a whirlwind of activity and movement that they choose either to resist or to submit to, but not to dominate. Ownership takes time to emerge: ownership over whatever they themselves create – the novel ideas, insights or perspectives that nobody but they could have brought into being. In an ideal event, the experience itself, the memory that the event leaves, is the sum of these insights. So the participants enter an event owning practically nothing, but they come out the other end owning a powerful experience constructed of things they've seen, heard or heard themselves say.

Coming back to the sponsors, how does their role change through the life of an event? During the run-up to the event, they become owners of the scope and content of the event and co-designers of the event's flow.

During the event, I avoid treating sponsors any differently from other participants. Should questions arise ("Is this really as simple as it looks?" or "How should we deal with that obstreperous participant?"), I pull a sponsor or two aside and seek guidance. I also ask them to stay behind at the end of each day to de-brief and challenge the next day's design in light of the day's discussion.

About two-thirds of the way through an event, though, when I throw the big questions back to the participants and ask them to define what remains to be done, I turn to the sponsors and pass the reins of control (or the illusion of control) to the sponsors, visibly and openly.

"Are you happy with where we are going?" I ask. "Are you comfortable with the way the participants want to structure their work for the rest of the event? Are you happy with how they've re-framed your questions?"

As the participants develop their own sense of ownership over their ideas and insights, my role as a facilitator becomes less necessary and, as such, less tenable. I transform into a simple moderator – time-keeping and the like – and almost ostentatiously shift the focus of work from myself to them. The participants need to know that they are working for the achievement of the sessions' objectives and outcomes, which by now have become *their* objectives and outcomes. The sponsors, who until this point have been without particular status, now need to provide guidance and assurance that what the teams are producing is, indeed, what is required. In a word, the sponsors assume the role of guide or leader that I had temporarily usurped.

At this point, the outcomes – and thus the design – belong to the participants and the sponsors. The 'co' in co-design has shifted from predominantly the facilitator's to becoming entirely the client's.

When It Gets Difficult

Sometimes this process of co-design gets off on the wrong foot. For example, a new client might come to me with a prepared agenda and say, "Here. Facilitate this!"

It isn't easy to coach event sponsors on what their role is – refining desired scope, objectives and outcomes, preparing the inputs – and what my role is – drawing up the map and blazing the trail. After all, they're paying and, anyway, they've held dozens of events just like this one and they know what they want.

So when they hand me their own draft agenda, I take a deep breath and listen very carefully as they walk me through their ideas. I assume that at some level they must have a good reason for constructing the event as they do, and I rack my brain trying to identify what that reason might be. And if I can't discern what they are after, I simply ask.

"Why do we need this particular presentation (or, more likely, cascade of consecutive PowerPoint presentations)?" I might ask. "What information do the participants need in order to do the work we're asking of them?"

Bit by bit, I manage to build an understanding of what the sponsors are really after, while assembling the ammunition I need to propose a more suitable alternative agenda. Good bedside manner, along with the judicious offering of very sexy alternative modules (simulations, scenarios, and the like) can usually win a recess until the next meeting when I can propose my own alternative.

(At this point, I should say that if an architect designing a house for me were to try this same stunt, I would fire him or her on the spot. So forgive my arrogance in knowing what my sponsors need better than they do, as well as my hypocrisy in not taking my own medicine.)

But what happens when the sponsors demand a structure or even a single module that is simply wrong? One that will move the event in the wrong direction or even undermine the sponsors' own position? I think there are two possible approaches.

The first approach is to express my doubts without proposing any alternatives. I save the discussion of my proposed solution until we are in my environment and therefore playing by my rules. Reviewing the entire event, including the sponsors' misguided ideas and briefly reiterating the doubt I had expressed earlier, I present my alternative version in context and simply hope for the best. This almost always works. When the sponsor-imposed draft reflects a broader failure in the overall structure of the event, a meeting with the sponsors in my environment at least a week before the event is called for.

But what if they dig their heels in and insist on doing the wrong thing? When I'm faced with doing the wrong thing, with delivering a module or an entire event that I don't believe in, and I can't back out, I take the Irving Berlin approach: I face the music and dance. I become my sponsor. I try as hard as I can to believe what my sponsor believes and never let on that I have doubts.

Is this hypocritical? Is this dishonest? I don't think so. I think that we often ask our sponsors to believe in us, to trust us to take them somewhere that they might not be comfortable with and that they might not even understand. And when they ask the same of us, it is only fair to oblige. Trust that only runs one way is a con job.

Facing the music and dancing doesn't always work. I have had modules and even events blow up in my face because I was unable to change my sponsor's mind and was forced to play along.

The most extreme case of this happening was when the sponsors thought they knew the answer to the way the final rounds of work should be designed and I accepted their solution – the CEO was adamant and I acquiesced (critical error number one). But during the synthesis conversation on the third day of the strategy event, the participants revolted against the ideas for how work should be done, ideas that I was now fully pushing (critical error number two). I resisted the participants' new way of dividing the work for about half an hour before I realized my two blunders. We ended up splitting the third day of work between what the sponsors wanted and what the participants wanted. I should have seen this revolt in the making days earlier.

Sponsors As Allies

Sponsors need to act as allies throughout the event. We don't always understand all the technical content and may need help keeping complex content straight. Understanding the sub-text can be even more difficult, since we are not privy to their culture or the hidden meanings and shorthand when they speak. If there is something we don't understand, we need the comfort to turn to the sponsor, whether in private or during a large-group discussion, and say, "I don't know what a 'HEDIS' gap is," without embarrassment. More importantly, participant comments or behaviors might need to be translated for me; seemingly-innocent comments often camouflage some back-story that I know nothing about. Periodic private sponsor de-briefs during an event can go a long way to building my understanding. By actively serving as my eyes and ears in the team activities and in plenary discussions, I can be more confident that I have the pulse of the group.

I also expect the sponsors to exemplify the sort of behaviors I would like all participants to exhibit. If participants see sponsors on the phone or otherwise distracted, they will know it is okay to be less than 100 percent 'present' in the event. But if the sponsors demonstrate their energy and enthusiasm and commitment, if they show up on time and switch off their phones, the other participants are more likely to do the same. Sometimes these demonstrations of enthusiasm are less than sincere. Fine. If we can assure constructive behaviors, we can get the work done and trust that genuine enthusiasm will result from a job well done.

The sponsors need to remain my allies even after the event is over. Effective value capture depends on, among other things, the sponsors' support to help us distinguish between signal and noise and to help translate the event's outcomes into an actionable form. (See Chapter 8, Value Capture.)

Over the lifecycle of an event, I probably invest two-thirds of my total time and energy in working with sponsors. I need to build their trust in me and I need to learn to trust them. It is an investment that pays almost certain returns.

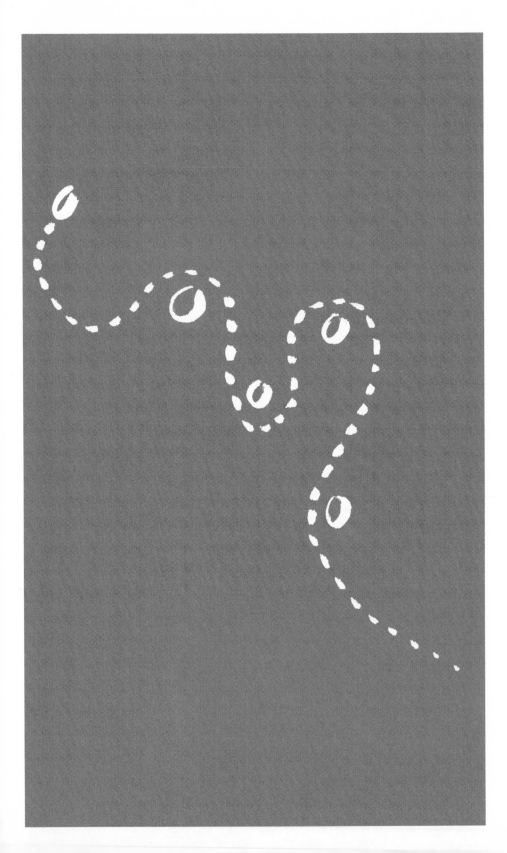

CHAPTER 5
PREPARATION

The tangible aspects of event preparation focus on logistics and on assembling appropriate knowledge inputs. We'll touch on both these areas, but first let's work on the intangibles, on learning enough about the client's issues to be able to ask the right questions and to be able to place the observations and insights that individuals make during the event into the broader context of the event: its narrative and its sub-text.

Client Interviews

I learn about the client's issues by reading everything they give me and through desk research, but above all through one-to-one interviews. Face time makes all the difference. I usually start with the sponsors, interviewing them individually, and then grow my 'sources' by asking to speak with more junior people, with 'dissidents', with line managers. When possible, I speak with the customers of my client or other divisions that overlap with my client's work. Within organizations, the political water-cooler talk can completely change my design approaches.

Colleagues occasionally ask to see the interview guide I employ for these meetings. Alas, I don't have one. I usually start by explaining who I am and the purpose of my visit and then I simply ask if there is anything they would like to tell me about the initiative or circumstance our event is addressing. Often I don't have to ask anything else; once the line of communication is open and the person I'm interviewing has the impression that I am genuinely listening, he or she opens up and tells me more than I ever bargained for. I take notes about the business issues and the actors who are involved. I am looking for multiple perspectives on the same issues, so I find that the more questions I ask, the less likely I am to hear something novel. I prefer the conversation to wander and I limit my role to asking follow-up questions; digging deeper when I don't understand something, respecting my own curiosity and the enthusiasm or fear or ambition or impatience arising from the issue at hand.

If third-party research about a client and its participants is available, especially if the participants filled in registration information or survey details, I scour these to try to understand the participant dynamics I am facing. In the ideal situation, I receive a network map of the relationships between participants so that we can make even more targeted interventions. Most clients have not moved into this data + design approach to collaboration yet though.

As I make connections with comments I have heard from other interviewees, I mention this, anonymously, and fish for reactions. "You mention that capital reviews are out of control. One of your colleagues mentioned that the delays are already piling up in your weekly sprints. What do you think?" I am not looking for confirmation; rather, I am hoping to accumulate competing opinions, so that I build as complete a view of the issue as possible.

What exactly am I looking for? Three things really: First, a 'map' of the client and the issue we're addressing. Second, a compelling hypothesis about the unspoken sub-text of the event. The map helps me understand what the client's issue *is* while the sub-text helps me understand what it *means*. Third, politics. I want my work to be a catalyst for real change. If I sniff dead ends I bring it up with the sponsors and even ask for additional sponsors to cover the political pauses.

When consultants speak of 'mapping' a client, they are usually referring to power relationships, influence, and advocacy. Mapping for me is much more subtle and difficult to describe. I compare it to the emergence of a mental map of a city as one comes to learn one's way about.

I've lived in several large cities – New York, London, Singapore and now Minneapolis – and when I first come to live somewhere new, I find my way by relying on a few known landmarks, on large streets

I've come to recognize, and by slavish reliance on the A-to-Z or later, Google Maps. When I first moved to London in 1989, I had a sense of where Hyde Park was and its relationship to Green Park and St James's Park, a general idea of the meandering course of the Thames, the fact that Piccadilly ran East-West – macro-features of the city's structure. Separately, I knew the theaters around Leicester Square, the museums in South Kensington. I knew that the City was to the East of all this and I had a sense of Fleet Street and of St. Paul's, but not how the individual elements fit together.

I spent weeks and months exploring, following the same streets by foot, by bus and by taxi. One day, from individual features, streets, and neighborhoods, a city emerged. In my head, the relationships between these isolated areas, the streets and monuments and shops and schools came together and then London made sense to me. London went through a phase change: from a growing collection of individual places, it suddenly gelled into a single city. Although my knowledge of London's streets grew gradually, my understanding of its geography came to me more-or-less all at once. To this day, to my amazement, I can still navigate my way from stations to landmarks and back again – often without looking at a street sign or name (or Google Maps).

While interviewing clients, I am after the same sensation: the accumulation of bits of knowledge until, magically, they coalesce into a coherent picture. And just as I explore the same streets by different means, so I solicit the same information from different people until the accumulated knowledge ripens into understanding.

And sometimes I discover maps layered upon maps. For a three-day event with a large healthcare insurance company addressing the quality of care and payments they receive for maintaining quality known as the STAR ratings, my interviews slowly revealed dynamics much more complex than the quality metrics and customer service metrics that were the ostensible objects of our work. This technical/logistical map was closest to the surface. The next map concerned the difficulties in collaboration between government priorities, insurance company priorities and patient needs. One level deeper lay another map describing the institutional rivalries, distrust and lack of faith between physicians, government agencies, insurance company interests and of course patients. Finally, another map emerged, one detailing the personal sympathies and antipathies that had developed over the years between the key stakeholders.

Of course, any event that is worthy of our time sports the same layered complexity that only comes into view after numerous interviews and extended reflection. This methodical surveying of the maps of our client's multiple issues is central to the facilitator's role.

When I work with consultants, especially those concerned about my fees and about their bright young employees whose timesheets they strive to fill with billable hours and learning experiences, they often ask whether I can delegate some of the event preparation to others. I appreciate their dilemma, but I am rarely able to delegate more than a mere fraction of this work. I don't use an interview guide for them to employ. It does me no good if the 'map' of my client emerges in someone else's head; it isn't possible to transplant that map into mine. And the individuals I meet and their quirks and peeves that I observe all ease my way into the event itself.

Research, Knowledge Objects, and Pre-work

While preparing for an event, I am simultaneously looking for as much input as possible and as little as I can get away with.

When participants have to learn on their own, I want to provide them with much more material than they can possibly digest. Abundance puts them in a position of having to filter, to decide what matters to them, what to make use of and what to discard. Making decisions about what is important keeps them in the driver's seat.

When, on the other hand, participants are in a passive position of being presented to, the less material the better. To keep participants in the role of protagonist in his or her work, I want them to 'receive' as little as possible of other people's knowledge; perhaps just enough to formulate smart questions and to be able to dig fruitfully for more.

Many sponsors prepare extensive pre-reading materials so that participants arrive better prepared for the work ahead. I try to discourage this. While I might want to bombard them with content *during* an event, I think that making them the passive recipients of knowledge without benefit of the context we create in the event itself is not productive. More practically, only a minority is likely actually to do the pre-reading. When they discover that the others haven't done so, it can poison the atmosphere. When the pre-reads are non-negotiable, I push to have a core categorized as 'must read' with the bulk sent separately as 'also useful'.

Sometimes, the best preparation is to do something rather than read something. For an event with the marketing department of a large financial organization, we asked participants to arrive at the event having visited a store they would never normally go to, and bring back proof or a prop from their visit. This preparation was much more pertinent than any reading list could have been, and participants came fired up and eager to talk about their experience. Having the prop added a new dimension and generated curiosity well beyond just talking about the element. For the record, I went to a MAC make-up store. I would never have guessed they gave out free specialty tools to help select and apply make-up.

With more restrained groups, I occasionally introduce the module through a 'live demo' by corralling a few of the more extroverted participants to act out the work before the larger participant group begins. In this case, standing in front of mostly white, male, older participants talking about my first cosmetics experience freed them up to be more animated in sharing their marketing experiences.

In addition to the information we send beforehand or what we ask them to digest during an event, we also surround participants with facts and figures, photos and articles, diagrams and headlines that they can refer to during an event, stumbling across something potentially useful wherever their gaze happen to fall. These 'knowledge objects' are essential to transforming any work space into a rich, learning environment in which ideas are shown respect and where serendipity is as important as detailed planning in determining which ideas prove important and which prove not to be.

Whether knowledge is shared on paper or through an experience and whether preparatory to an event or during one, putting the participant in the position of choosing what is important and finding his or her own meaning in that knowledge is the key that will make that knowledge impactful. As Plutarch wrote, "The mind is not a vessel to be filled but a fire to be kindled." Our job is to build the fire and light the match.

Logistics

There are countless books and guides on event preparation focusing on logistics, venue selection, and set-up, so I'll stick to the few principles which I believe make the greatest difference: Space, Light, Sound, Stuff, and Food.

Space

I want all my participants to be *present* – right here, right now. That means having enough space to have all my participants in the same room throughout our time together. No break-out rooms, please!

When participants are all together in plenary and are then sent off to break-out rooms, the awkwardness seems to last forever. First they need to figure out where they're going – maybe down the hall, perhaps upstairs. Once they've found where to go, there is that unpleasant silence while people take their seats, stare at one another, and figure out who will have the courage to start talking. It can take ten minutes until the energy and intent with which they were sent to their break-outs is re-created. It's all so painful and unnecessary!

Keep everyone together. Keep the plenary and the break-outs in the same large room. Break-out areas can be defined by flip-charts or work panels. Plants make an enormous difference. When there is sufficient budget, I use large rolling work panels which take dry-erase markers and are magnetic.[8]

To keep everyone together in plenary and in break-outs requires 75-100 sq. ft. per person; a bit more for smaller events, a bit less for bigger events. Lots of freedom, nothing bolted down, no incline, no stage, NO WALLS, though a few pillars are OK.

---

8   A simple summary of great collaborative white boards for every budget is available here http://bkle.in/21Zxz2g

Light

Lots of it. Natural light helps people feel good about their work and reduces fatigue, though direct sunlight can be a nuisance. Strong, uniform artificial light helps them see their work and see each other.

Sound

Good acoustics make an enormous difference. If people can't hear each other, they can't collaborate. We want as acoustically-dead a room as we can find. That means carpeted floors (yes, even the outrageously ugly carpets that most hotels seem to prefer are worth the assault on our eyes – I am still looking to fund a Kickstarter campaign for the first ballroom carpet coffee table book!), curtains (keep them open, though), and ideally an acoustic ceiling.

If the acoustics allow it, you *always* want to avoid using microphones. They slow you down (passing them around) and they reduce intimacy. But if you must, you must.

Regardless of whether I will be using microphones, I always want a first-rate sound system to be able to amplify music. In Chapter 7, I'll expand on the importance of using music as a facilitation tool. For now, suffice it to say that an excellent audio system is a necessity. If your venue isn't forthcoming, rent one.

Stuff

Yes, you'll need supplies, you might need equipment, you'll certainly need chairs (two per person, one for plenary and one for break-outs), maybe a couple of tables (for supplies and coffee cups, *never* for participants to sit at), some technology (printers, big screens, Wi-Fi...). Don't scrimp.

Food

Catering is not a detail. Sharing food and drink together is a fundamental element of collaboration and has been since before humans had language. Furthermore, eating together can reduce the tension that frequently accompanies events on important topics.

The quality of the food and drink we offer can either support our work or get in the way of it. Good, healthy food fuels our participants and should be chosen with care. Workshops can be stressful and consequently people may eat more than they otherwise would. So keep it healthy... and abundant. Water works better than coffee to keep people alert. Please don't allow turkey lasagna for lunch. It can be more detrimental than a bad sponsor.

These five elements – Space, Light, Sound, Stuff, and Food – will have an enormous impact on the ability of our participants to get the most out of our work. We tend to think of logistics as being of secondary importance. Getting the logistics right won't make up for a badly-designed or badly-facilitated event, but the best-designed and -facilitated event can be so easily undermined by poor logistics.

So it's doubly mysterious that hotel meeting services tend to offer exactly the opposite of what we need:

Space: Hotels often avoid providing floor plans or divulging square feet. Their calculation of room capacity is based on counting chairs in a classroom or cabaret set-up. It's usually about a third of what we need. Then they pile on the break-out rooms, which are of no use to us.

Light: They often have dingy chandeliers and offer black-out curtains so your projected slides are easier to see. No thanks!

Sound: The acoustics of the rooms they offer is sometimes acceptable, sometimes not; what's surprising is how architects and hotel staff seem so uninterested in whether people can hear each other. In terms of amplification, hotels are very accommodating, as this is a high-margin ancillary service they provide.

Stuff: How unusual it is to find light, stackable, comfortable, attractive chairs! Why is it so expensive to rent a photocopier? And at those prices, why doesn't it *ever* have paper inside?

Food: Lots of pasta and sandwiches and sugary snacks. How about more fruit and vegetables? Oh, and please serve things I don't need a knife to cut.

Facilitation Team

When I was a boy, I was frequently told: "always hold hands when crossing the street," and the lesson has stuck with me. I would never go to a client meeting alone and I would *certainly* never attempt to facilitate an event alone. The question of Ecosystem Management (see p. 2) lies somewhat outside the scope of this book, but this is not to minimize the importance of having an appropriate team of colleagues to support an event.

The mix of people I look for tends to be determined by the design methodology I employ. In the case of the MGTaylor DesignShop™ approach, the following roles are typically foreseen[9]:

Facilitator: usually me, and the object of this book.

Graphics: including developing a 'look' for the event and, above all, graphic facilitation.

Production: ensuring that inputs are in the right place at the right time, as well as archiving participant work.

Documentation: capturing plenary discussions in real time.

Environment: keeping the space fit for purpose.

Music, Video, Photo, Research: as the names suggest.

Process Facilitator: managing this team (including the facilitator) and the broader ecosystem.

Data Analyst (for large events): managing participant/content data plus networks of people to ensure accelerated knowledge transfer.

There might be several people playing each role or each person might have to cover several roles. The important thing is that the

---

9   For a more thorough look at team roles, visit http://bkle.in/1Pxjzpi

roles are defined and people know what they need to do and what they can rely on someone else to do.

Preparing for an event means imagining what will be asked of each role and ensuring that the right people have been invited to support the event.

I like big teams. The interplay between the team members is fun and the ideas that emerge are so much better than those that a small team dreams up. And as a facilitator, I need to know that I'm surrounded by colleagues who have an idea of what is going on at any particularly moment and, more importantly, *why*.

Even with hundreds of events under my belt, I still sleep fitfully before any complex event. I toss and turn in bed in a state of near-panic: "I don't know how to do this," I say to myself. But then the morning comes, I meet the team for breakfast and I breathe a sigh of relief. "Of course!" I remember, "I don't *need* to know how to do this. The team knows."

CHAPTER 6
DESIGNING

As I wrote in Chapter 1, this book is not about design. There are many outstanding methods and tools for building effective agendas and planning impactful workshops. Rather, it is about *facilitation*, about the face-to-face interaction between a facilitator (collaboration engineer, change-agent, transformation manager, what have you) and a group of people with a shared goal (participants).

Yet design and facilitation are not separate realms. The design choices one makes – before and during an event – and the way one behaves while working through that design are closely, though never perfectly, aligned.

This chapter is about those attributes of design that I am unable to extricate from the in-the-moment experience of facilitation. In particular, I am thinking about two things:

Iteration and recursion
How the same themes emerge in different contexts and at shifting levels of detail.

Common language
The use of metaphor and of learning tools to help participants discuss their concerns in unexpected ways and establish a deeper dialogue.

In addition, I'll touch on the way participants experience our facilitation and how this should influence our design decisions, as well as on several facilitation challenges whose resolution can be found in thoughtful design. Finally, there is a moment in some events when facilitation overtakes design, or when the two merge in the most unexpected and profound ways. This moment is called *emergence*.

Iteration and Recursion

Meeting agendas are usually linear; workshop agendas must never be. A meeting addresses a series of topics, usually addressed in order – what the historian Arnold Toynbee would describe as "one damned thing after another." This linear structure serves to help people remember the past but inhibits thinking about – or creating – the future.

A workshop's structure has to reflect the exploratory nature of understanding and of the creative process. The meaning we intuit and the meaning we create both depend on a process of discovery. First we see outlines, then shapes, then color and depth and texture. The activities woven together to design a workshop are never free-standing. Each contributes to the whole and none has much meaning divorced from that whole.

Dictionaries define 'iteration' as 'repetition'. As a design and facilitation imperative, iteration is *not* repetition. In our context, iteration involves trying to answer the same question in many different ways, from new vantage points, with evolving language, and with a shifting cast of characters.

For example, during our time with the leadership of the Young Global Leaders (see p. 40), we examined the approach over and over again, each time from a radically new perspective. In one round of work, we investigated each person's individual initiative. What short- and long-term goals did the individual have? How could their experiences enrich the journeys of fellow community members? In another round, we broke participants into zones of a marketplace. Mimicking a real-life flea market, but with vast amounts of data on each 'stall', we were able to engineer the most beneficial stalls for each person to visit during their time at the market. We then asked each person to make at least three contributions to the stalls they visited. In another round, we sliced up the data of people giving support and asking for support and followed Wharton Professor Adam Grant's principles to facilitate connections between people to develop even more collaborations.

Each of these rounds of work represented a different 'lens' through which to look at the participants and the mission to dramatically enhance their conversations, yielding more impact on improving the state of the world. Each round raised issues that overlapped or conflicted with issues raised in previous and subsequent rounds. None of the rounds 'solved' the problem of the session itself or even the wider mission, though in each team discussion there was likely to emerge at least one small insight that might survive to the next round to be incorporated or adapted to new uses according to who introduced it into the novel context posed by the next round's challenge.

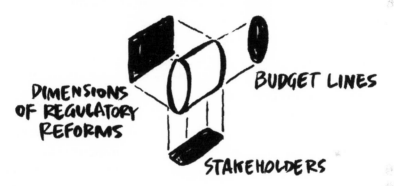

These are all examples of iterative design. *Recursion* moves beyond iteration and introduces the concept of scale. To continue with the example of the Young Global Leaders meeting and its strategy, we might shift our focus of investigation to the scale of the individual participant. We might examine how he or she makes their way through five years as a member of the community, identifying all of the ways that he or she might interact with the Forum and its ecosystem and how those interactions might promote or undermine learning, networking and collaborations. In another module, we might take a step back and look at how such a small community (~900 members) impacts the wider world or even impacts the city chosen for their next meeting. We might ask participants how their day-to-day work could be integrated, even though their jobs have nothing to do with the community. These dimensions might emerge as disciplines (e.g., How will the communities' research impact the scientific community? How will its educational approaches affect the health of the nation and the world? How will its community graduates make the world a more just place?) or they might emerge as concentric circles on a globe (e.g., How should the community impact every town its members live in? What should that town expect from such a direct link to global thought leadership? What should be the community's impact on its region? Its country? The world?).

Another level of recursion might shift us to the metaphorical. In almost all of the YGL community events, we choose multiple metaphors. Before going all out on metaphors, I usually recommend first-time sponsor teams and facilitators to start very simply. For example, many companies are looking to improve customer service. Rather than having participants talk about it – or even worse, ideate on it – design an agenda where they go and meet a customer service rep from Nordstrom, or sit with a call center agent from Zappos. Better still, have them spend a day with one of their own customers. Even spend a day as an Uber driver (provided you don't have a criminal record, you can easily become one for the day).

Collaborations among this exceptional group of under-40 year olds could make a major impact in reshaping the world. Choosing the right metaphors can make a big difference to their discussion. One of the earliest examples to shape the community from within was by using other organizations as metaphors for how they wanted their community to develop. Such 'metaphorical organizations' could include an orchestra, the Church, a rebel movement and so on.

An orchestra is perceived as a single body and is judged by the single sound it produces; yet it is made up of soloists, many of whom are *prime donne*, under the leadership of a conductor with very few tools to rely on. Its financing is precarious yet its patrons are wealthy. It is closely associated with the city in which it is found. It aims for an inchoate excellence, somehow associated with a collective interpretation of a hundred-year old score. Without sublime collaboration, its best talents are wasted.

The Catholic Church is both a discrete (with defined boundaries) and universal institution. It exists as an ideal of God's perfection yet operates in man's world of compromise and earthly banalities. The Church embodies an ancient hierarchy, and a collection of buildings each with its own architecture, artworks, and maintenance requirements. It represents a community of people who identify with it to one degree or another.

Rebel movements: these are both scalable and tribal. They often exist to resist current state power structures and compel devotion until death. Their leadership can be distributed, but their common cause is enough to topple entire nations through their passion and perseverance. They may purport to create the optimal future for a group of people yet they often cause the very problems they are fighting against.

Common core communities: from True North groups inspired by former Medtronic CEO Bill George to Weight Watchers™ groups, these short- and medium-term groups assist members through placements or periods in life and can have transformative effects on the mental state of an individual. Yet their communities are often small and short lived.

Hackathons: not really organizations, but small groups of people trying to rapidly solve short challenges. Originating as computer coding, they have been adapted to fit any type of challenge. Eager participants push forward not just solutions, but actual prototypes, working programs or processes. By their very nature, they are short term and their outcomes, no matter how good, are up for dismissal often within minutes.

We introduced this metaphorical recursion during the first day of a three-day event. It began with a lunch-time reading assignment. Without offering explanation, we provided heaps of books and articles to dozens of teams, with multiple participants per metaphor, and asked them to learn as much as they could about their assigned topic while helping themselves to lunch. Depending on the metaphors, we may also use TED talks, magazine articles, research papers and more to elicit the same responses. For the orchestra team, we provided work on musical composition, orchestral direction, and the memoirs of the late conductor Herbert von Karajan. For the Church teams, we provided books on ecclesiastical law and church architecture, and several copies of Saint Augustine's *City of God*. The rebel movements team got everything from American Revolution stories to the tactics of Pablo Escobar. Each team had far too much material and the individuals would need to choose what was potentially interesting to them.

We asked them to read quietly while they ate and then asked them to compare notes on what they read. No questions about YGLs. Finally, we wheeled out their coats and told them that buses were waiting, without telling them where they were off to.

The orchestra teams naturally talked to members of an orchestra plus other musicians in different types of groups. For the church teams, several members of the community were monks or priests and the teams visited different shrines and places of worship. For rebel (or rebel-like) movements we were lucky enough to be in Myanmar (Burma) where the groups got to meet Aung San Suu Kyi, visit members of her team and even visit her house. For the different types of communities metaphor, participants met with student groups at Beijing University as well as with university leaders trying to engage the next generation of Chinese leadership. Members got to talk directly with Bill George and discuss forming some True North groups. All participants explored different types of small groups within their community. We even experimented in creating a group comprising all bankers. It failed. All artists – failed. Half artists and half bankers – failed. But when we put one or two artists together with several bankers, it produced amazing results.

After an hour or more of discussion with their hosts, we brought all teams back to the ballroom where we asked them to apply what they had learned about their assigned metaphor to the community as a whole and how we could create more successful collaborations together. There followed a series of conversations of enormous substance about ways of communicating, about funding of ideas, about the relationship between the Forum, partner organizations, members, private corporations and governments, about the status of alumni; in short, all the issues that the community had been facing for years, but had been unable to address directly. What the metaphors provided was a new way to talk about old issues and barriers. Without their site visits, they would have repeated the same ideas, efforts, ways of working they've been having for years; instead, the metaphors provided a new language – a common language – with which to have a new conversation.

These multiple levels of recursion provided an appropriate entry point where each participant could engage in the variety of options they had created to help improve the state of the world.

There is a more important aspect to recursion, which relates to the integrity and internal coherence of a model or a solution. It is not the objective of this book to address systems thinking, which is what this type of recursion refers to, but suffice it to say that a systemic problem will affect an organism or an organization at many different levels or scales; a systemic solution will likewise be applicable regardless of level or scale.

Themes & Metaphor

As I work on the design of an event, a particular metaphor usually presents itself as being especially effective at reflecting the various dilemmas that the event intends to resolve as well as the underlying, unspoken paradoxes which make finding a solution without our help so difficult. I grab hold of this metaphor and translate it into an overriding theme for the event as a whole.

For example, in the case of 14 organizations being brought together mentioned earlier, I felt throughout my interviews that there was an underlying tension between the current ideal of each individual entity – a place of localized excellence – and the day-to-day reality of demanding patients, budget changes, regulatory confusion, technology changes (mandates), the expectations of local employers, and the constant rotation of leaders. For this reason, we chose the theme of Monopoly. Not only has everyone played the game, but the variability of Monopoly properties was a perfect fit.

We created 14, six-foot wide Monopoly boards with interchangeable pieces that we converted over the course of three days to represent multiple elements. The first day, it was the game of meeting your competitors (14 acquisition companies). Players had to invest in winning strategies (by selecting Monopoly properties). On the second day, we introduced Monopoly money, with the CFO's face in the middle, raising the level of the challenge to include profitability across all properties. On the final day, we abolished the rules, challenging each participant to realize that the collective group was more profitable and successful when they worked together. The event continued with investments and financial plans focused on the deliverables, but the theme remained throughout, allowing players not only to have fun, but to eliminate their acquired identity and become team players.

We used Monopoly as a visual theme for the entire event, ultimately creating a 40-foot wide version of the real plans to integrate the organizations.

During the event's opening I shared my personal Monopoly story. When studying abroad in Germany, I learned to despise the game. Not because of Monopoly itself, but because the host mom served asparagus for every meal and the exchange house only had one bathroom. Enough said. Without asking, you could watch participants' brains turn on and reflect upon their past. I spoke for less than a minute and yet rekindled hundreds of memories, smiles or reflective smirks on participants' faces.

What I never did was *explain* the theme we had chosen. A small number of participants might have strung these clues together and drawn conclusions about our intentions, but I am confident that the vast majority noticed few if any of the references we employed. That was just fine. The point of choosing a theme and then plumbing its depths to find visual, textual, musical and conversational counterpoints for their work is not to be *understood*, it is to be *experienced*. Metaphor can provide an intellectual thrill when deciphered consciously, but, when it enters through the brain's back door, so to speak, metaphor provides something more profoundly new: perspective, new language, insight, surprise. Metaphor (*transport* in Greek) transports participants to an unexpected place from which they can survey their own world and its issues from a new perspective.

We choose a theme for almost all our events and almost never

Some Examples of Event Themes

Event Description	Theme
A three-day event for HP on transforming the organization	Transformers (yes, the children's toys)
A marketing department integrating dozens of products	Ecosystems and their infinite loops
A company integrating 14 acquisitions	Monopoly
Reversing the cost trend for healthcare in America	Mission: Impossible (yes, from the movie)
Re-designing Wired magazine's tech influencers to improve the power grid	Power to the People

choose the same theme twice. We usually put great care into choosing the theme, as we do for choosing whatever metaphors we employ, and as with metaphors, I am convinced that much of this effort is wasted. Any metaphor would probably work, so long as it is open to multiple interpretations. Except for the few who enjoy our choice of theme at a conscious, literal level, the majority will take what they need from whatever theme we were to choose. A theme is like a rough-hewn lens; participants will polish it to correct their personal myopia and serve their own particular needs.

Facilitating versus Teaching; Creating versus Learning

Any time a group of people spend time together, they learn from each other. And whenever we bring people together to solve a problem or create something new, they need to learn new things – ideas, language, tools, perspectives – to do so.

But even though people need to learn things in order to work with us, that doesn't mean it is our job to teach them. On the contrary, our job is to facilitate that learning. First consider the fundamental behaviors of a facilitator and those of a teacher. They both spend much of their day asking questions, but with utterly different expectations. A teacher will rarely ask a question without already knowing the answer; a facilitator should *never* ask a question if he or she already knows the answer.

A teacher's purpose in querying participants is to share knowledge (which the student who has been called on might know; otherwise the teacher provides the answer) and to test how prepared the students are.

A facilitator's question, on the other hand, is grounded in curiosity. A facilitator really wants to know why medical plans can't be as simple as cell phone plans. A facilitator wants to know why, based on archaic contracts, a million dollar event required me to collect $10 at the lunch line from each participant (so they could enjoy a soggy tuna melt). A facilitator simply wants to know why your customer experience isn't as simple as Uber's.

These questions aren't intended to teach; they're intended to help the facilitator – and through the facilitator, all the participants – to learn what the issues are and why their solutions are not obvious.

When knowledge transfer is a necessary element of our events, we find mechanisms other than 'teaching' to help participants absorb what they need to learn. We put people into small teams to learn from each other – with or without an 'expert'; we provide posters, books, articles, and pictures for people to sift through and decide what is important; we send them into the field to do their own research. In sum, we put knowledge in their way and let them stumble over it. We don't teach.

Templates and the Search for Questions

On the last day of a large event, sponsors asked that we provide the participants with templates to capture and structure their work. We acquiesced.

What did we gain and what did we lose by using templates? We gained two things principally. First, the sponsor was pessimistic that all of the necessary details would be captured by every team... and felt comforted by the thought that she and her colleagues would, at a minimum, fill in the templates with useful information. So we helped lower her blood pressure for a few hours.

The other benefit of using templates was the uniformity of output, which simplified the design and production of an executive summary. If all participants are working to the same template, building a deliverable is a cakewalk.

The downsides of using templates far outweigh these benefits. First, the uniformity of structure rarely corresponds to the variety of issues and ideas that emerge from genuinely creative work. Second, providing templates robs the participants of some of their sense of ownership over their outputs and thus of their event.

But the most damaging aspect of templates, I believe, is that they represent a pre-formulated question. As an event proceeds, our questioning should leave more and more room for interpretation. Early in an event, we strive for some sort of elegant ambiguity in our assignments to leave plenty of room for interpretation, and as the work proceeds, our assignments become so short and open-ended as to offer barely any guide at all as to what is expected. We do this because the answers our participants provide are only a fraction as useful as the questions they have to ask themselves to arrive at those answers. The most creative aspect of their work – and thus the most difficult – is figuring out what the question is that they are trying to answer. When they stumble and go around in circles and lose their way, it isn't because they don't know the answer, it is almost always because they don't know the question. And *the search for a question* is the most genuinely creative aspect of collaborative work.

One way to make templated outcomes more useful is to have the participants design the templates themselves. In an event for the NonProfit Organizations Knowledge Initiative (NPOKI – a collaboration of non-profits including the Bill & Melinda Gates Foundation and the World Health Organization, that is trying to improve knowledge and systems to improve care-giving), we were asked to provide templates to teams in order to better capture the individual elements of knowledge-sharing decisions. We designed two rounds of work in which teams were asked to identify the minimum information needed to make the required local, national, international and technology system decisions and then to design templates to capture this information. We then mixed the teams and had them refine the templates and settle on three designs, which the participants felt would simplify their subsequent collaborations.

Using these 'home-made' templates in the final work round provided structure which helped simplify the next steps, while still leaving participants the necessary room to ask the questions that mattered most to them.

The 'Right' Design

We put so much effort into developing the 'right' design, the one that will transport the participants to the place they 'need' to be, that we rarely consider the infinite number of designs we didn't propose. It is true that we design and re-design and re-design again before and during almost any event we facilitate, but once the event is over, the design we actually ran seems to be the only one that could possibly have led to the outcomes we achieved. But there's more than one way to skin a cat.

I was working with the strategy unit of a large consulting organization. It was a delicate assignment since the unit was run by two old-timers – who had very strong opinions and who didn't like or trust each other very much. Their behavioral issues had infected the entire unit, which was consequently struggling with direction.

Yet the questions this pair were asking were great questions: How do we measure the effectiveness of our consultants? What exactly is our 'product' and what is the optimum balance between *push* (providing guidance and leadership) and *pull* (responding to the stated needs of internal clients) in our offering? How can we make our work more valuable? How can we make it re-usable? How do we decide which products and people to invest in? How do we decide how to compensate employees based on company direction, not just on past products and services that are still selling nicely?

I worked on a design that unpacked these difficult questions and gave the participants the opportunity to discover their own solutions and to re-engineer the way they created their work products and interacted with their clients. I thought that the behavioral issues should be addressed off-line through coaching and that anyway, a more focused team would decrease the importance of these leadership issues. I was proud of the design and felt that it could make an enormous difference in the effectiveness of this strategy unit.

But then a week before the event was due to begin, my second daughter was born. Luckily, I have extremely dependable colleagues and one of my partners, Tom Kehner, offered to step in. I informed the two sponsors and gave Tom a thorough briefing. I had been working with this client for years and Tom was new to them and indeed to the whole healthcare ecosystem (he is an engineer by training). I walked him through the design – I had even written the assignments – so all he really had to do was step into my shoes and run with it.

Of course, you can't step into another facilitator's shoes. In those few instances when someone has handed me a pre-designed event to run, I am unable to deliver this design. I mutiny and create my own. Without consulting me, Tom did the same. He delivered a fundamentally different event; one in which he addressed the leadership issues head-on. For him, the question of how the unit functioned was unresolvable without a top-down re-think and that's the event he designed and delivered.

The event was wildly successful and had a lasting impact on this unit. When I returned, I debriefed the sponsors on the event and their experience working with Tom. We didn't discuss the original design – there was no point – but the new design brought out issues that they had never considered and created the opportunity for a different sort of transformation from the one I had understood they were looking for.

The fact is, they needed *both* events, Tom's and mine. They delivered – or would have delivered – different outcomes and all those outcomes were important. Most of our clients need the events we facilitate for them, and they need another ten events too, each different from the next. But they usually only get one for any particular issue.

Does this mean we assign too much importance to the particular design we end up facilitating? Perhaps it does.

Emergence

Although this book does not address the design of an event (i.e., the shape of the agenda), we have discussed at length the process for arriving at that agenda. The next chapter looks at how we deliver an event; that is, how we as facilitators behave when we are at the front of the room and participants look to us to understand their own role and to learn from each other. There is, however, an in-between space, where an event's design, the process for creating that design, and the in-the-moment facilitation of that event come to resemble each other. This in-between space is where *emergence* happens.

Emergence is a term that describes how highly-organized structures can result from extremely simple or even random components; for example, how very simple insect behaviors, when taken together, achieve a rich social structure; or how the wind and waves can shape millions of grains of sand into intricate patterns of ripples and dunes. Just as complex structures can emerge from simple building blocks, so too, important insights can emerge from discussions that appear to address much simpler issues.

Our most successful events reach a critical moment of creative energy and collaborative focus when things just *happen*. Ideas flow, participants genuinely listen, a large gathering achieves an intimacy normally experienced only by a tight group of friends, unexpected insights come tumbling out of contributors' mouths, one idea after another. In these rare moments, teams discover their true potential and make remarkable breakthroughs.

But emergence cannot be engineered: there is no workshop agenda with a few hours set aside for the 'emergence module'. In fact, the more linear the agenda and the more it drives towards some specific conclusion, the less likely that emergence will occur. Rather, our job is to create space for emergence, assemble the necessary ingredients, and, like scientists creating life in a test tube, apply energy.

In an event for the Arab League and their Arab Thought Foundation, they asked us to lead their annual gathering at their headquarters overlooking Tahrir Square in Cairo. At first we resisted. The League had remained largely unchanged for 70 years (it is older than the UN). Finally they said that many of the leaders would acknowledge that they had failed to achieve their goals in helping to create a better union of the 22 nations the League represents. We agreed to support them as long as they would let us train 55 local facilitators and 15 graphic scribes, half of whom were women, to lead the event. My colleague Antoine Viorney flew back and forth to Cairo half a dozen times, meeting with presidents and princes to create a design that was 'emergent' – one that left room for the unexpected – because there were so many elements which we simply could not control.

We knew Arab countries had some of the most hierarchical structures on the planet, but the importance of emergent design was never so critical. The League has had countless Westerners come in and tell them what to do – all based on what has worked in the West, or how great democracy and the Internet are. We knew we couldn't come in with a traditional design and continue to perpetuate the same agenda. So instead of teaching how to facilitate, we listened. We asked questions. Co-designing with the prince and the 55 young (25-35 year old) facilitators, we wrote breakthrough assignments. We challenged: if a Saudi Arabian leader wouldn't listen to a young female facilitator in a break-out group, we would pair her with a man and instruct him not to speak. If they wanted to put a template on the wall to provide structure, we would let the facilitators and participants do it. Afterwards we would discuss the results. All 55 new facilitators agreed to avoid templates at all costs in the next round of work.

Most interestingly, all of our work, once complete, was sent to the communications department to be translated into Arabic and then printed. We never knew what they actually said. But we developed a rapport with the young facilitators to guide their senior country leaders on the path of emergence to open their minds.

We focused on security and culture; youth and the social economy; development and finance. We intentionally didn't solve anything. We were there to further open the conversation in the hope of achieving collaboration. We found ourselves on the news in most Arab countries with photos of commoners and kings mingling in break-outs with young female facilitators. We facilitated discussions reportedly unheard of within the sacred halls.

During the design process, our job was to resist a linear, step-by-step design in favor of a more recursive design that could allow participants to discover unexpected linkages and insights. In the design itself, we built in as much variety as possible, both in terms of the

topics discussed and in terms of the levels of recursion that these topics were viewed from. As facilitators, we tried to create the right physical and psychic spaces for such a discussion to occur. The physical space consisted of chairs in a circle, so that participants could see each other and so that what would otherwise have become a simulated discussion of individual comments and insights had the chairs been facing the same way, emerged as a genuine conversation. With the 55 facilitators, we ended up on the floor – arguing topics and ideas and ways we could lead the event together. The psychic space was created by ensuring that shy or low-status participants were encouraged to speak and by acknowledging their ideas and capturing them on white boards. Through body language and occasional repetition or re-phrasing, we maintained a high level of energy in the room, but otherwise we played no role whatsoever in 'guiding' the discussion; our job was simply to let it happen.

We can't design for these fortuitous moments of emergence, and they don't happen in every event. But we have to design every event and facilitate every debate in a way that increases the likelihood that such powerful discussions and such important insights will emerge.

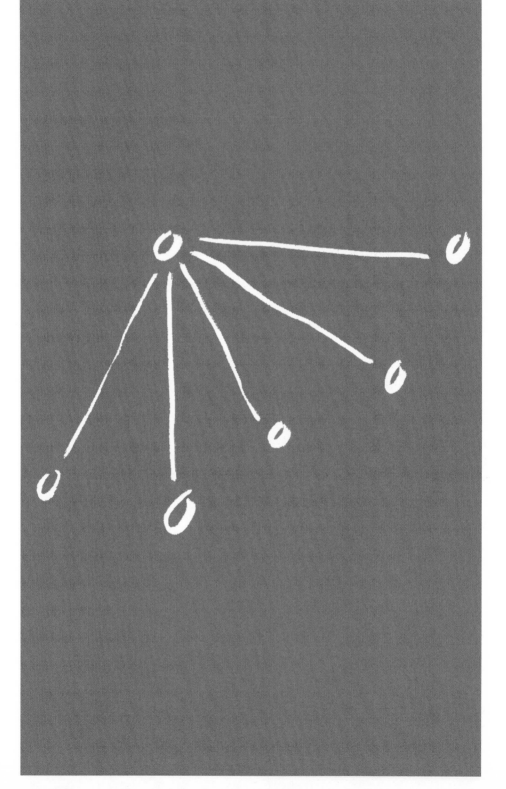

CHAPTER 7
DELIVERY

By *Delivery*, I mean, how we as facilitators behave during an event. Whether we are at the front of the room waving our arms about, or at the back of the room nodding our head to encourage a team representative reporting their work, or wandering around from team to team, eavesdropping and commenting – how can we be most effective?

WHY WE DO THIS

The purpose of this book is to investigate how we facilitate the interaction of large groups of people who are trying to address a common issue. But we can't understand the *how* without investigating the *why*.

Why ever would we invite dozens of people, all with busy schedules, to take time out of their lives to work on a question together? Nobody really wants to commit the time and nobody really likes workshops anyway. Let's not even start talking about the cost! What are we hoping to achieve?

I often have difficulty untangling the *how* of our work from the *why*. When asked about the nature of our work and what 'facilitation' really means, I find that I repeat a few stock phrases that have entered my lexicon and I too rarely stop to ask myself what they really mean:

"We help people have a new conversation about old problems."

"We give people a chance to listen to each other and to feel that they were listened to."

"We play our client's games, but by our rules."

"We guarantee that they will get more done in three days than in nine months."

...and so many more.

All these definitions are true and I think that they each have real substance, but it is perhaps only the first of these three that begins to touch on the *why*. We help people have new conversations about old problems.

"Make It New"

So many of the issues we are asked to work with have lain unresolved for years. An event immediately after the passing of Obamacare legislation serves as a case in point. The relationship between the elements of the healthcare delivery system (e.g., patients, physicians, drug companies, hospitals) and the divisions that oversee them (e.g., legislation, insurance companies, the FDA, consumer rights advocates) had dogged healthcare for decades – perhaps centuries. While the catalytic event that brought all the players from the healthcare system to our door was government reform and its financial implications, any lasting solutions would have to address this underlying conflict.

Yet the topic was so old, so hackneyed that genuine dialogue had ceased ages before. So the underlying *why* of our event was to allow them, finally, to have a new conversation about this old, old topic.

A more recent event for Time Warner illustrates this issue. The event was originally devoted to tackling online piracy, but with participants from different regions and access to lots of trend data, the event quickly became about how to deal with the rise in online video from YouTube, Netflix and more. While the debate revolved around content ownership, cable networks, DSL versus fiber-optic lines and licensing rights, genuine dialogue around how the consumer actually wanted to watch films had regressed into the background. The issues that really needed discussing had merged into the baseline condition of the company and were the frequent object of chatter but almost never the basis for genuine dialogue. The language for dialogue had been polluted and degraded; it no longer had meaning. People talked about complexity, but they had stopped saying much of value years earlier.

> *Tching prayed on the mountain and*
> *Wrote MAKE IT NEW*
> *on his bath tub*
> *Day by day make it new*
> *cut underbrush,*
> *pile the logs*
> *keep it growing.*
>
> - Canto LIII, *Ezra Pound*

Our job was to create the conditions for having a new conversation about the reality of the changing market dynamics. The environment, the team composition, the design, the graphics...everything we built was intended to eliminate the old ways of talking about the excessive complexity that had infected the organization over the years and to let them see this complexity, and talk about it, in a new way.

So I believe that the principal role of the facilitator during an event is to *make it new*. Make *everything* new.

We know how to do this. We listen to what people are saying and try to re-phrase it in more precise language. We write down what we've heard so that people can see it and not just hear it. We apply our most critical judgment; critical of ourselves so that we always leave open the possibility that what was just said was both true and important; and critical of the participants so that we tease out unspoken assumptions and challenge them, no matter how reasonable or widely-believed they are.

We take advantage of being outsiders to ask the ignorant question that no one else has the courage to ask. We share a politically-incorrect observation that many are thinking but none dare say. We interpret. We mis-interpret. We tell stories.

Storytelling to Make the Conversation New

I wrote at some length in Chapter 2 about the importance of story-telling as a fundamental facilitation skill. Here I want to touch on when stories help and when they don't.

Stories serve to provide new language and new imagery with which to diagnose a condition or circumstance as well as to imagine alternative realities. In a 50-person event with a major strategy division, we told the story of the making of foie gras. The division was going through a significant transition and the rate at which teams were 'cramming' ideas, PowerPoints, strategies, organizational changes, layoffs and more was out of control. We felt it was pertinent to acknowledge the problem might not be fixable, but as a collective group, we could make it a lot better.

The foie gras story fell flat. Very flat. No one cared. It was forgotten immediately. I think it failed because the link to our event was one-dimensional. Yes, transitions need to be overseen and some of the finest food on the planet is as good a story as any to turn to, but it just wasn't enough. Our stories need to work at multiple levels of recursion; they need to have meaning whether observed through a microscope, a telescope, or with the naked eye.

What does the strategy of one of the largest healthcare providers in the country mean for the workers and their families? What does it mean for the rest of the company and the shareholders? What about for how people move and think about healthcare? What does each person's life mean for making the world a better place? Why should the stories we tell be a metaphor for this company and its strategy?

Perhaps the foie gras story did have the depth and detail necessary to support this kind of storytelling, but we never dug deep enough to find out. Had the story been able to offer this sort of richness and complexity, we wouldn't necessarily have had to make all these connections and un-pack the food at each level of recursion. The *possibility* of finding multiple meanings at different levels of recursion is sufficient to keep people's interest and, more importantly, to provide a lens through which to find something *new* about their strategy and the stories they will need to tell themselves and each other in order to make the transition successful.

During a different event – this time for a parent company trying to translate its corporate values into employees' behavior, product attributes and business processes – we told the story of historical icons, such as Mohandas Gandhi, Henry Ford and Harriet Tubman, highlighting the misdirection, failures, course changes and personal barriers they had to overcome. Not only did I discuss some of them in front of the room, but we covered the environment with photos, quotes and stories about their lives.

I felt that the mirror this story held up to the parent company was multi-faceted – as if the mirror had shattered and each jagged shard provided a slightly different vantage point from which to judge the value of their values, so to speak. It was a simple story but I felt it had relevance at multiple levels of recursion:

- Values are more than slogans.
- Change is about actions rather than words.
- Culture (and thus any value) can be present in superficial ways and absent in more fundamental ways.
- Failures (in the case of the healthcare sector, bankruptcy and death are all too common) can be more likely and more devastating due to the complacency that results from slavish repetition of values.
- Inconsistency between values offers an opportunity to discover their deeper meaning rather than being an embarrassment to be ignored.

I didn't have to explain my story and all its possible interpretations; I merely had to provide enough detail to leave open the possibility that even a minority of the participants would seek more meaning than the few issues I'd sign-posted in order for the story to be successful.

And how do I know it was successful? Because over and over again during the subsequent two days, participants adopted the language or the imagery from my story in order to tell their own stories. Their concerns were not particularly new – they had been working on values for quite some time and they were indeed a sore point at certain times – but the story I gave them provided tools with which to have a new conversation about old issues.

Overcoming Barriers of Fear and Status

Another use for telling stories is to say what otherwise can't be said. As my colleague Chip Saltsman says, our job is to "find the fear and go there." Our job is to ensure that people genuinely listen to each other, and fear can make that impossible. Stories can create the possibility for telling the truth metaphorically, without fear.

In an event for the Texas Medical Association (the largest group of physicians in the USA representing 48,000 practicing doctors), our event objective was to modernize and improve navigation of Texas's broken health system. We wanted to avoid the old discussion of insufficient resources, lack of pricing transparency, too many legal constraints, physician burnout, disengaged patients and so on. So instead of telling a story, we demonstrated one.

We had two members of our team sit at the front of the hotel (the ballroom was at the back) with a photo of each participant. They then radioed back to two other team members at the front door of the ballroom who had their first assignment for the day prepared. Instead of the doctor just finding their nametag and then filling in information from the assignment, our team already had their nametag in hand and greeted the doctor personally. There was some mild shock, since the doctors didn't know our team, but we knew their names and immediately engaged with them as honored guests. Our team walked each doctor over to another doctor that they already knew (People Science) and made a subtle comment about their medical specialty and related it to the challenge or assignment they had in front of them.

By taking a light-touch approach to what was in fact a serious problem for physicians in Texas – by exemplifying a story rather than continuing to talk about what could be – we gave them the room to tell similar stories to each other and experience personalization previously unseen. From the moment they walked in the door, they let their guard down and allowed themselves to share openly with the other 85 doctors in the room. Yet, had we not invited them into the story, giving them a voice to speak honestly about the shortcomings of their industry, they would not have had the tools to fix these shortcomings while developing their collective strategy going forward.

One year earlier, we designed and facilitated a large three-day workshop for HSBC and their senior leadership. We were developing long-term objectives for sustainable capitalism in the age of industrial change and the modern sharing economy. The purpose of our work was to help leaders develop the stories that they would like to hear 10 years from now, focused on:

- relationships
- sustainable capitalism
- talent development

We divided these topics into storytelling devices:

Focus on Relationships: each participant told a story about their network and how they leveraged it for good. Then we provided a network map of the strength each person had with their peers (this People Science approach shows connectedness and flow of information between colleagues).

Sustainable Capitalism: we had them tell a story about their physical environment at the office, at university, in their charity work, in a start-up garage, and other incredible environmental experiences they may have had. Much to their surprise, we then asked some of them to sit on cardboard and recycled wood and bamboo chairs. Two of the participants rode electricity-generating bikes to generate the power for lighting the room. To top it off, we published the source of each material we used in the room. Do you know the carbon footprint of your coffee cup? Or how the footprint varies if it's paper, aluminum, plastic, ceramic or glass? Do you know how many parts of your chair were transported more than 4,000 miles by an oil-guzzling ship?

Talent: we had them simulate being the next generation. Each person played another person from a different demographic in an online digital community. Positioned around the space were large cutout people imitating live actors because the client rejected having outsiders listen in. I wish I could publish the conversations that ensued. A 48-year old Dutch banker, mimicking an Indian school child texting 50 words per minute while trying to take public transportation to school, is priceless.

There is also a fine line that you have to be careful not to cross. During one event about how to redesign intelligent medical systems to predict potential health outcomes, some of the participants, who knew that I liked to make my events new, decided that the best way to get groups from different divisions working together was to do an *a cappella* version of singing Chihuahuas. They were amazing. So amazing that it fully shifted attention away from the purpose, therefore derailing the event. They crossed the line and I let them do it.

One of the most complex series of events I was ever a part of involved hundreds of 'languages' (languages in this case are the countless medical codes used to describe each and every medical condition, plus the laws governing them in different states). The US Government reimburses healthcare companies based on the risk of the patients they are managing. For patients, this can mean significantly improved care compared to what they were previously receiving, while for doctors and healthcare providers, it can mean more money to do their jobs better (they have to spend their own money on the patients). New technologies can analyze tens of thousands of patients simultaneously and identify patients at risk. This is great tech, but the patients actually have to be seen by doctors. So reaching out to patients, communicating with them and getting them seen for their risk areas is a phenomenally complex task. You have to simultaneously work with thousands of physicians and nurses, hundreds of companies, countless bosses who have different priorities and more. In a series of workshops, we had to get everyone aligned with standard ways to approach the data, then reach out and do the assessments to help both the patients and the companies.

The final piece of language was the different legislation across states. All of these issues had to be delicately addressed by the group. We used visual facilitation and giant process maps created on ballroom floors since hundreds of feet of air walls were not enough. We kept running lists of different words that meant the same thing. We kept charts of common diseases and used computers to auto-match where the overlap made a difference. Thankfully, all of this information was uploaded so that the computer could translate the different languages, acronyms, diseases and properties automatically.

Our participants frequently speak different languages, using different acronyms and assumptions. They believe that they share a language, but listening to them carefully reveals that they do not.

Armed police states are thankfully few and far between, but strong-arm enforcers who inhibit free expression are part of almost any participant group. We think that hierarchies fade away under our respectful facilitation, but we are fooling ourselves. And who has facilitated an event in which an IT department and its internal customers need to hammer out a service-level agreement, without encountering paralyzing illiteracy?

The fact is, the very facilitation tools we need to employ in what appear to be extreme circumstances are precisely the tools we should be using every day with every participant group. The fundamental barriers to collaboration are the same – fear, unequal power, lack of understanding, unwillingness or inability to *listen* – and the same creative approaches should be employed to overcome these barriers regardless of context.

I will never forget driving in south Florida last winter with my four-year old daughter. She asked where we were going. I responded: "Miami". She laughed at me and asked me again where we were going. "Miami", I repeated. She finally said, "but it's MY-ami, silly dad, there is no You-ami. Where are WE going?" My, me, you, our – ami? How wonderful.

THE CENTRALITY OF COMMON LANGUAGE

As I hope these examples show, our ability to help participants discover or create a common language is fundamental to the success our work. Likewise, the absence of common language makes genuine understanding impossible and sabotages our work.

The easiest way for a large group to avoid taking a difficult decision is for it to use language that people can interpret at will. Imprecise language, euphemism, cliché, and 'flexible' interpretation lead to the illusion of consensus – or acquiescence – whose battle cry is the ubiquitous, exasperated, and exasperating "Whatever".

In an event for the City of Tucson and one of their largest hospitals creating one of the country's first Accountable Care Organizations, the lack of common language nearly prevented participants from understanding what they were agreeing on and why such agreement might really matter. It's easy to agree that, for example, "all hospital reimbursement payments will, from now on, be managed by a separate reconciliation organization in order to maintain stronger population health in the city." But it's altogether harder to agree with this statement if we haven't defined the precise scope of 'reimbursements' and haven't agreed to what a 'reconciliation organization' is or is not, who runs it, or how it will be held to account. Giving participants the tools to develop their own definitions of these terms and the space to work out and document the precise meanings of each element of their models proved to be key to the success of the event.

Even in shorter meetings, this is still critical. In an event for the World Economic Forum at their annual meeting in Davos, Switzerland, we facilitated a session with global leaders on the sharing economy. Except that, what is the difference between the sharing economy and the creative economy? Or the gig economy? Or the circular economy? Even the shut-in economy...

It is easy to agree, for example, that "all independently-employed individuals will now be free to fend for themselves where government and corporations used to service healthcare, retirement, community, unions and more." But to understand the implications at city, national and international levels, we started the session by giving every small group exactly the same set of materials. Straw, balloons, candles, sticks, wire, glue. They had to physically build what the new economy would look like and define how the items would interact. They had to label each element and then tell a story about how it would all work together to make a better planet. Before five minutes were up, princesses, CEOs and nobel laureates were stringing yarn across the room, using candles to inflate (and pop) balloons, laughing and cheering along the way, simultaneously creating a common language and understanding – the balloons representing the economy kept popping as they tried to figure out the new model for the sharing economy.

Helping participants to build models is nearly always part of any collaborative design process and a model isn't complete until its elements have been accurately labeled. In both the Tucson and World

Economic Forum events, the principal outcome – a detailed operating model – was accompanied by a highly-detailed glossary and a set of precise criteria for defining new elements that might enter the model in the future.

Multiple Languages

What languages do we have at our disposal?

We have a modeling language that helps participants construct alternative futures and test them. The modeling language gives participants the courage to be precise and avoid compromise. Interestingly, when we teach our modeling language, we start from the most basic elements as if we were teaching German or Swahili. We begin with lines, dots, and shapes and then build a modeling grammar and vocabulary that participants can use to paint remarkably rich pictures.

We have a pattern language[10] which helps us shape and model collaborative behaviors. Very little of our pattern language is codified, but that doesn't make it any less precise. I find that the most remarkable consequence of our pattern language is the speed with which our teams, frequently made up of people who have never worked together before, can know the best way to behave in novel circumstances.

We also use a musical language in our events and too often underrate the precision and power with which music can transform a difficult-to-enunciate emotion into a shared and remembered experience. The words of the songs we play rarely make a useful comment on the work we are doing. Much more important is the music itself, both for its ability to harmonize our energy and for its remarkable power in touching parts of our psyche that words never reach. More about music below.

It is metaphor that provides us with perhaps the most powerful

---

10   The MGTaylor DesignShop™ methodology contributed enormously to our profession by, among other things, translating the concept of Pattern Language, developed by architect Christopher Alexander to the realm of collaborative work. See http://bkle.in/1SvdA9b. There is also a new book on Pattern Language from the Collaborative Code by master facilitator Rob Evans

language of all. I discussed the centrality of metaphor as a design tool in the previous chapter. Metaphor is also essential as a front-of-room facilitation tool in order to create common language.

Storytelling is, as we have seen, a key facilitation technique. I choose my stories carefully (though I almost never plan them in advance) and having told them, I return to them for the rest of the event as a source of metaphorical language. When we introduce metaphors during large-group discussions or during team exercises, we enable our participants to mine these metaphors for new language with which to see their problems in new ways.

The flip side of metaphor is simile, and we need both. Metaphor is useful when we need to open up a topic, when we need to see a problem from multiple and unexpected points of view. Simile, on the other hand, is useful when we need to develop more precision in language.

What is the difference between metaphor and simile? Here is T.S. Eliot comparing simile in Dante to metaphor in Shakespeare:

> There is a well-known comparison or simile in the great XVth canto of *Inferno*… He is speaking of the crowd in Hell who peered at him and his guide under a dim light:
>
> > *…and sharpened their vision (knitted their brows) at us, like an old tailor peering at the eye of his needle.*
>
> The purpose of this simile is solely to make us *see more definitely* the scene which Dante has put before us…
>
> > *she looks like sleep,*
> > *As she would catch another Antony*
> > *In her strong toil of grace.*
>
> The image of Shakespeare's is much more complicated… "catch in her toil" is a metaphor. But whereas the simile of Dante is to make you see more clearly how the people looked, and is explanatory, the figure of Shakespeare is expansive rather than intensive; its purpose is to *add* to what you see…[11]

---

11   T.S. Eliot, "Dante" in *Selected Essays, 1917-1932*, London: 1932, Faber & Faber.

So while the precision of simile can be useful for painting a picture, it is the transformative power of metaphor that helps us to look at the familiar and see something completely new.

I facilitate events in both the tech world and the regular world. I say this because it has an enormous impact on how I facilitate. In some ways, my mother tongue is technology. Although not a coder, I can be more precise and historical in the tech world than any other industry in which I facilitate. From the time of my first laptop computer in 1986, I was hooked. While my friends watched movies and played in their free time, I would read about technology trends and new development languages. My journey in the art of facilitation began in 1998 with a three-day DesignShop™ session to determine the merger between Compaq and Digital Equipment Corporation. The consultants working the session as subject-matter experts didn't quite understand how a member of the facilitation team could know so much about both companies' products. In some respects, this is valuable because I can help participants by providing them with richer language which they can accept or reject, thereby adding precision. In other industries, I often ask participants to re-phrase their comments until they reach a level of clarity that I am comfortable with. In sessions requiring a deep level of industry expertise (often the case in the bowels of healthcare), I explain my uncertain interpretation of their comments and ask them to help me understand better what they are trying to say. In technology, I am the language's master; in everything else I am its slave!

Each industry's language presents intrinsic challenges. For example:

- Government agencies are prone to acronyms. I had top secret government clearance for two years with a few Department of Defense and other military contracts. No one would continue reading this book if I listed the many acronyms used by these agencies.
- The worlds of conferences and corporate education are dominated more by logistics execution and their own special language, than by honest discourse and true change.

- Lawyers abound with irony. They live in the world of law by the letter of the contract, but they don't practice it in collaboration. They bill by the hour, so they have less meetings, but are more verbose than an overzealous cable news presenter. They write contracts so difficult to understand that it's no wonder they find it hard to collaborate. They have more jokes about their profession than anyone else... and they deserve it.

- Banking...where to start? For several years, I worked in Broad Street, New York, where we could see the Stock Exchange as we walked between break-outs and plenary discussions. We used to play the game Four Square in front of the Exchange façade. This was in the post-9/11 days, so there were no cars. Artists, shopkeepers, laywers, police women and more would come and join us. The bankers, however, would clutch their ties and walk by. But then we realized it was simply a matter of refreshing the language of the game. We just had to say there was a prize (ROI) for whomever could stay in the 4th position (Four Square King spot) the longest. Boy, you should have seen the line-up of bankers eager to play after that! Inside the scope of facilitation though, the language of phrasing the objectives is even more critical for bankers. We ran a two-day event to redefine the consumer's ATM experience. Our event design was nothing special, but to get the bankers in the room engaged, we simply shifted the language of 'consumer-friendly' to the need to shave eight seconds off the average customer experience at an ATM, which would in turn save $x million for the bank. Give a banker that and a Martini and you would think Sisyphus just gained a robotic exoskeleton and ATMs were finally cool again.

- Finally, consultants. Perhaps the most special breed of all, since I still consider myself a 'recovering consultant.' No other language that I am familiar with has as many buzz words and meaningless sentences to sound hip as my fellow consultants' language has. In one session for Elmers (a company that owns, among other brands, Krazy Glue), we were trying to create new products for the next century. But there were so many buzz words that I overheard one Elmers employee blurt out: "If anyone says we need to get on the same page again, I will Krazy Glue your face shut!"

In summary, my ability to demonstrate that I precisely understand what participants are trying to communicate – that I am genuinely listening to them – is a proxy for their desperate need to be listened to by one another. Precision in language is one of two prerequisites for helping clients know they are being listened to. The other is actually listening. And oh how much easier it is to listen with care and attention when they speak with care and attention! A large part of our job is helping them to do so.

PLOT AND ENERGY

Twenty years ago, I started a dotcom focused on natural and complementary medicine. I started it because my mom had a rare disease for which conventional medicine wasn't able to offer any support. It was a type of dystonia called 'spasmodic torticollis'. We built the company to 65 employees and retailed 22,000 different products, including providing a platform for 50,000-plus healthcare professionals to communicate and improve patients' lives like my mom's.

However, it wasn't until several years after departing the company (some investors made a lot of money when part of the company was sold to Tesco Plc. and some just had a great experience) that I realized my biggest lesson. *Every bit of advice someone told to me was true. I just had to experience it in order to be able to apply it successfully.*

One of the early mentors that helped me understand this also introduced me to the art of improv and story-telling in order to succeed. One example – very simple and incredibly easy to follow –changed how I facilitate. It was based on the work of the storyteller Robert McGee. I had always thought of a story as the line connecting A, the beginning, with B, the end. A, my mom got sick. B, my mom got better. What I learned from McKee was that stories are nothing like this.

Stories are a succession of scenes in each of which the protagonist is faced with a decision, great or small, and the choice the protagonist makes reveals the nature of his character. In the 2015 film *Bridge of Spies*,

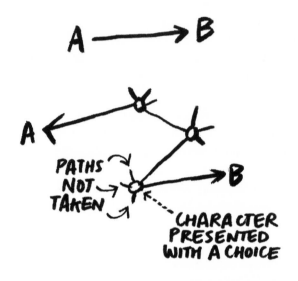

Tom Hanks's character refuses to accept the prisoner exchange of a U-2 spy plane pilot, held by the Russians, for a KGB spy, held by the Americans, without also including the American student Will Rogers in the trade. Acting against the orders of the US government, Hanks puts his life at risk, yet persists, thereby revealing his loyalties and true good nature. At the end of the film, when the final trade of prisoners happens across the Glienicke Bridge and Checkpoint Charlie, Hanks refuses to accept the final transfer until the student is safely in American hands. In those and many other scenes, the characters are presented with novel circumstances and the choices they make in the heat of the moment determine whether the plot goes this way or that. So a story is not a line connecting A to B, the beginning to the end, but rather a scene-by-scene sequence of divergent paths, and the path that is chosen reveals to the audience – and to the protagonist himself – the true nature of his character.

Keeping the Event Moving: Divergent Paths

I think about the first company I started and McKee's lessons in story structure when I design an event and even more so when I am facilitating one. My job is not to get from A to B, from beginning to end; rather, it is to make use of each module, each transition, and each conversation to help the participants discover the true nature of their business, their project, and their character as a group. They make these discoveries when, at every moment in an event, we reveal to them that the path they are on is actually made of choices; they are *always* at a crossroads and we create for them the freedom to choose which path to take. One hospital CEO pulled me aside halfway through an event and said, "Is this a trick? It feels like you're sending us out on a mission to solve healthcare each time the music plays."

When the leaders of the New York Daily News lost themselves in a discussion of declining newspaper sales, I waited until the energy was just about to wane and then I asked about demographics, or terrorism, or the economic cycle, or millennials, or the currency markets... *anything*, so long as they challenged their linear way of thinking and saw themselves as facing choices. And how they resolved these choices helped them discover who they were, what their strategy was, and what the likelihood was that they would implement that strategy.

I don't actually know much about the newspaper industry or about demographics, terrorism or currency markets; but I do know a little and with what little I know, I listen for clues in the things the client says in plenary, in break-outs, and in informal conversations. So when I present them with a scenario that transforms their linear A-to-B discussion into a succession of trade-offs and choices, I try to use their own language, their anecdotes and imagery to help them recognize the richness of the conversation they could be having and to remove myself as much as possible from appearing to have a stake in the outcome, which I scrupulously do not.

Sometimes a different avenue can present itself when the facilitator's mind wanders and lands in an unexpected place. While facilitating a sponsor meeting for responding to the passage of Obamacare focused on hospital management (see page 90), I was getting lost as they spoke about how their hospital and insurance functions were structured differently from that of their chief competitor and government requirements. I listened patiently and tried to make sense of what I was hearing, and then, when the energy was about to seep out of their discussion, I facilitated an escape – just as Tom Hanks had done for the American student trapped in Berlin.

I made an observation that only someone who knows nothing about hospital management and even less about healthcare law could make: I commented that their cash cow was running on antiquated systems ill-prepared for the future of consumer-focused healthcare, while their competitors' products (including the most downloaded iPhone App and physician-friendly system integration systems) were much more customer-facing. As you can imagine when someone criticizes someone else's baby, the room went silent and hostile gazes turned my way.

The lead sponsor asked whether I had read the new healthcare law and, when I admitted that I had not, he casually dismissed my impertinence. He and the others were about to move on when one of the more junior sponsors piped up. "He might be right," she said. "We're the market leader now, but companies X & Y and others are way ahead of us in key areas." And then they began talking about what consumer healthcare change might have to do with their legacy healthcare integration businesses. Without any further provocation from me, they reached a much more brutal conclusion than I ever could have. They realized that the way their business currently operated comprised of a billing system for consumers, a population health data set disconnected from anything, a hospital revenue management system, and a bunch of tentacles that 'talked' separately to their consumers. They didn't even design for the patient getting better, they concluded with long faces, but rather individual subsystems that the patient/consumer would probably never figure out.

This sort of self-flagellation wasn't at all my objective, and of course they did then dial it back a bit. But this critical observation served to raise what became fundamental questions about how the hospital was integrated across a patient's health (god forbid that every bit of healthcare would be delivered in one hospital!). I had opened an alternative pathway – a patient-friendly one – and the sponsors wandered down it and discovered new ways of talking about complexity and simplicity in hospital management.

In music, ambiguous chord progressions or unresolved harmonies create tension that makes the music more interesting to listen to. Chord progressions have their own logic – they seek resolution – and even a poorly-trained ear, when hearing a particular chord progression, can guess what the next chord ought to be. Yet when a composer confounds that guess and leaves the progression unresolved, the music becomes interesting enough to listen to. When we are in the front of the room facilitating a discussion, it is the same. A discussion has its own logic and our job is to minimize the friction and the barriers that would interfere with that flow... until the time comes to introduce an unexpected chord, an unanticipated tension, an alternative path, thereby creating a choice for the participants as to how *they* want to resolve the discussion. And, like Robert Frost, who took the road less traveled by, we help the roads diverge, and that makes all the difference.

Levels of Recursion: *Escaping to a Higher (or Lower) Order*[12]

Perhaps the most important way to open up a divergent path is to be far enough away from a conversation to identify the level of recursion at which it is taking place, and then uncover alternative levels of recursion to which it might shift.

If participants are talking about, say, empowering youth in 400 cities in 169 countries (a topic I recently facilitated for the Global Shapers community), the facilitator steps outside the scenario and imagines different levels of recursion to help re-frame the issue. Just youth? What about ageing generations, grandpas and grandmas? Just empowerment? What about the daily challenges of life? Just high-performing kids? What about the disadvantaged, the disabled, the technologically-poor? What about illness, or poverty, or loneliness?

---

12   Thanks to Gail Taylor for this turn of phrase and for the encouragement always to look for that escape.

In a series of small events in the USA focused on micro-finance organizations – including participants from World Vision, one of the largest global non-profits, Care, Finca and many more – we were tasked with imagining innovative technology platforms for delivering services to very poor children in developing countries. Having spent months on the ground, living in the homes of amazing human beings funded by micro-finance, I had a very jaded perspective of jet-setting international participants into meetings, however collaborative I might be able to make them. Nevertheless, participants began to hone some technical attributes that this platform would require. They came from a variety of organizations and many were recognized gurus in this specific realm (I will leave aside my bias that nowhere within 4,000 miles was the perspective of the recipient to be seen or heard). It was a constant challenge to keep them from rushing to conclusions. Finding the 'answer' too soon would close down the possibility for finding alterative answers and for developing the tools they needed to critique these various answers and refine them in constructive ways.

As these technical discussions moved forward (and again I am reminded by what an asset my ignorance can be) I would observe that a shrinking group of participants were discussing the issue in an increasingly animated way. These zealots were reaching important conclusions and taking real pleasure in discovering their own ideas by having to express them coherently to the others. One could see their peripheral vision shutting down, the way a predator's does when closing in on its prey.

This is a critical moment for a facilitator. Let the discussion continue? Interrupt the flow? Re-direct? Solicit input from others? In these emergent, creative moments, the stakes are extremely high and the facilitator's bias should be to do nothing; to listen, to give that assurance that people feel listened to, but to *do* nothing.

These discussions follow an energy curve – shaped like a bell curve. Our job is to remove the barriers that stand in the way of the apex reaching its potential and to recognize when the apex is reached and how the marginal value of each additional comment begins to decline, and with it, how the energy begins to seep out of the room.

It is exactly at this moment that the facilitator's intervention has

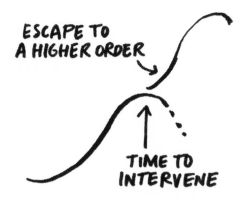

ESCAPE TO
A HIGHER ORDER

TIME TO
INTERVENE

the potential to add value, to create energy, and, in rare moments, to help the group escape to a higher order.

When I felt that the technical discussion in the micro-finance solutions event had gone far enough (not as far as it could have gone, but far enough to pass its peak), I searched for different levels of recursion at which our topic could be discussed. I didn't want to change the subject *per se*, I wanted rather to change the *nature* of the same subject. I wanted to change the 'fractal scale' of the conversation.

By the time I decided to intervene, a small number of highly-animated participants were talking about donor selected or controlled micro-donations (Kickstarter for development projects). At what level of recursion should I offer a question?

- What sorts of recipients should we be planning for that can pose challenges?
- How do the donors know what is a good project versus a bad one, or one that has been tried and doesn't work in that region?
- Who else might this approach be useful for?
- What other ways do people interact that might benefit from this approach?
- By putting the recipient and donor directly in contact, it solves several problems. In what other ways can distributing money, knowledge, power, information, resources, who-knows-what-else, benefit these people?

- If this approach is valuable for the world's poor, might it not also be valuable for us? How could we employ this approach universally and what would change if we did?

I could have asked any one of these questions and it would have had the desired effect: shifting the level of recursion of the discussion and by so doing, creating the possibility of escaping to a higher order.

Around the same time, I was facilitating an event for a Fortune 25 company on organizational design. The company had developed so many innovation departments and internal design firms, you would think that IDEO, Stanford Design School, Tesla and the venture capital firm Andreessen Horowitz all decided to vie for power in one company. Unfortunately, most of what it achieved was to confuse the internal customers they were trying to help by selling or giving away their services. In a plenary discussion early in the event, we were working through individual corporate functions and brainstorming design principles for each function to interact together. As the discussion proceeded, I noted that the comments shifted back-and-forth between what functions should *be* (size, degree of autonomy, risk-taking...) and what the functions should *do* (activities, interactions...). When I felt that we needed to escape to a higher order, I asked: "What is the relationship between what a function is and what it does? How does being relate to doing?"

This philosophical question is almost unanswerable and indeed we never did answer it. But the question caused the participants to step back from the detail they were lost in and consider the more fundamental variables they should be designing for. When we then sent them into teams to document their proposed design principles by function, we came up with a much richer result. Because my difficult question had helped them see a higher level of recursion, it was easier subsequently to fit their various design principles into an overarching framework. The *being* attributes of one function could be aligned with those of another function; likewise for the *doing* attributes.

A very simple and charming example of multiple recursions can be found in a recent 15-second advertisement for Apple's Siri on the new iPhone[13]. I will leave aside that Google's technology is far superior here to illustrate this point. The actor Jamie Foxx is standing in front of a mirror holding two movie scripts which he evidently must choose between. "Hey Siri! Flip a coin!" Siri responds, "Tails," and Jamie chooses the corresponding script.

It's a lovely ad that works at so many levels of recursion. One level is Apple's intention to demonstrate a Siri feature and its integration into daily life. But there are so many other levels:

- How do we make choices?
- What does it mean to make a random choice?
- How do we reflect on our desires? (Jamie is in front of a mirror.)
- Who is Siri? Is she in the phone or an extension of our will? Or an escape from responsibility?
- What is a script? Jamie is holding two scripts but is acting to a different script that Apple gave him.
- Does it make a difference or is his a false choice?
- and so on.

The point is that in a 15-second scenario, an explicit narrative (demonstrate Siri) offers us so many opportunities to search for alternative meaning, to change the subject, to insert new energy, to escape to a higher order.

I believe that when we are in the front of the room facilitating a discussion, we must *always* be listening for opportunities to shift the level of recursion of that discussion. We may only choose to do so very rarely, but at any moment, we must be able to see these different levels and then, perhaps, with care and humility, act on what we see.

We can see these alternative levels of recursion precisely because we are not part of the discussion, we stand outside it and in our heads we play with the context in which the discussion is unfolding. These occasional interventions, I believe, constitute our single most effective tool for channeling the energy of a large group discussion. We propose

---

13   see http://bkle.in/24kUObg

alternative levels of recursion so that a particular topic continues to evolve and involve as many minds as possible. Occasionally these shifts in level of recursion enable the participants to escape to a higher order, to see their issue or imagine a solution from a radically different vantage point. This is when the fundamental insights emerge.

Keeping Our Distance

I've spent more than a month of my life in 19 different cities. After a few weeks' staying in a new city, there's a moment when its geography gels in my head. From that moment on, I'm not a stranger there anymore and there's no going back.

With clients, the same moment arrives sooner or later and it is a problem. We learn our way around the corridors of their culture and we greet friendly faces at the coffee machine. We lose our objectivity, we stop asking the stupid questions, we mistake our knowledge for understanding. We can be of use so long as we don't understand anything. It is precisely our *struggle* to understand that helps our clients to turn their insight onto themselves.

A few years ago, I found myself, together with a new colleague, a novice, working with a client to design a second event. We'd held an earlier event during which I'd learned a great deal about the subject matter (development of a sales strategy across 11 different divisions for a newly-formed sales and growth office). Our second event followed two months later and we jumped head first into the design process, discussing objectives and outcomes and trying to figure out how best to make use of material that they had prepared.

There had been some tension between me and this client during the previous event (one of them was my boss) and I wanted to be particularly accommodating. I thought I understood where he wanted the project to go and I saw my job as helping him get there as effectively as possible.

Yet there was something deeply wrong with the objectives he laid out for us. They simply didn't add up. My colleague, who was new to this area, saw the incongruity at once: a mismatch between mission and strategy that was so much more evident from a slight distance than from the inside. Yet in no time I had moved sufficiently inside my client's organization and structure that I missed it.

As facilitators, we are not our client's colleagues. There is so much we will never see or understand about our clients and their business, but the few things we can help them see more clearly are only visible to us because we are strangers. That distance is one of the most valuable tools we possess. Whenever possible (usually budget dependent) I invite another facilitator to join me on events or at a minimum at least one member of the team that is incredibly perceptive and very experienced. These individuals have helped me out of numerous sticky situations simply as an outside observer.

Being Outside The System

As I mentioned at the beginning of this chapter, one way to describe our work is to say that we play our clients' games but by our rules. The rules we play by include our design for the event, the way we behave as facilitators and as a facilitation team, the environment we create for them, the music we play, our habit of breaking *their* habits; in sum, our way of working.

We keep hold of these rules as much for their own effectiveness as to deprive our participants of their own set of rules, their own behaviors and ways of working, which might be effective for the day-to-day running of their business but which are wholly unsuited to transforming their business. Otherwise, why did they call us in?

Yet the game remains firmly in our client's hands – the playing field, the scorekeeping, deciding who is a player and who is a referee, who is a spectator and who is a sponsor. Our rules; their game. And it is precisely because the game is *not* ours that we can be effective facilitators.

The game that the client brings us is a complete system. Its various moving parts all fit together, for better or worse. It has inputs (people, money, resources, ideas...); it does something with these inputs (designs, builds, manipulates, assembles, disassembles...); and it has outputs (products, services, money, a reputation, social impact...).

When a system (a client, say) is going through some sort of

transition, it attempts to build alignment among the components of that system. People who are part of that system design this transition and make plans to see it through. But because they are part of the system, they cannot really see it as a system. They tend to see the individual elements that make up the system, but the whole is invisible to them.

So a system (the same client) may call in a consultant. The consultant sits on the edge of the system, extending her roots and feelers through the system to collect data, to analyze, and to manage change. The consultant can 'see' the system more effectively because she is at the periphery and has a valid sense of boundaries and limits. But the true nature of the system remains invisible because there is no perspective from the surface, just recognition of a few local features. Likewise, bringing about change is difficult because, once the consultant's roots have taken hold, she can change the system only by changing herself.

The facilitator, on the other hand, is completely outside of the system. Only at this distance can the system come into focus. It starts to make sense as a client *and as a system*. We acquire unique value to the client by scrupulously keeping our distance, by being outside the system.

Yet at this distance, our relationship with the system, with the client, relies on signals and feedback. We detect things, we hear messages, we witness behaviors, and then we react, sending our own signals and messages and behaviors back to the system. At this distance, we have two surprisingly indirect ways to effect change and both depend on how we react to the signals we detect.

Quite simply, when we detect a signal – when we observe a message or a behavior that we believe adds to the discussion – we can amplify that signal. We repeat it, re-word it, draw it, fish for reflections on it from other participants – we try to inject it with energy. These are messages that add to the discussion, not necessarily those that we agree with or that we believe take us closer to what the sponsors told us the end point was. They are merely messages that we feel contribute variety, nuance, deeper meaning, or a contrasting view.

On the other hand, when we detect a signal that we believe detracts from the discussion, one that reduces the richness of the dialogue and subtracts energy from the room, we can attenuate that signal. We acknowledge the speaker (the nod of a head, eye contact, a grunt...) and then we move on. We might turn our back subtly or change the tone or volume of our voice. We try to break the flow and inhibit the feedback that this potentially destructive signal might generate from the group. By destructive, I mean not that we necessarily disagree with the speaker's sentiment, just that the flow of conversation that we believed was constructive is being inhibited.

So our two tools are to amplify constructive signals and to attenuate or interfere with destructive signals. And it is only our judgment – our evolving understanding of the dynamic of the group and the way our antennae wiggle when something's not right – that tells us what to amplify and what to attenuate. The power of the facilitator to amplify and attenuate signals that the system is sending to itself is enormous, and that power demands real responsibility. Since we float outside the system while a consultant lies on its surface, we could imagine that our power to influence that system is inferior to the consultant's; but quite the opposite is true. It is precisely because we are outside the system that our powers of perception and influence are so remarkable.

SETTING PATTERNS

We take participants out of their offices or meeting rooms, which they've frequented a thousand times, in order to break the patterns that emerge in those places. The patterns they normally adhere to might be useful for facilitating ordinary things; but our task is to do extraordinary things and the patterns that *we* exhibit – behaviors, habits, tools, processes, language – have to be extraordinary as well.

Or perhaps our patterns are the ordinary ones, the normal ones, while the tribal customs of typical group meetings are the weird patterns. Why do the substantial conversations only happen during coffee breaks? Why do people insist on making those PowerPoint presentations in a darkened room? They must know that nobody is following them! Why does the boss speak last? Or first? Why is the room so dark; don't they want to see each other?

These are the mysterious patterns that will take generations of anthropologists to decipher. Our patterns, in contrast, have a simple purpose, which is to facilitate discussion and alignment and emergence.

So our job is to live our patterns as if they were normal, because they are. I find that a good rule of thumb to follow from the front of the room is:

- *Never apologize!*
- *Never explain!*

Our way of work doesn't require explanation or apologies; it's those typical meeting behaviors that do.

Before we move on, I think it is important to remark about the next generation being brought up in bad corporate patterns. I was riding in a town car from Pasadena to Los Angeles airport trying to pitch a change-transformation series of sessions to the CEO of a large bank (it was the only way I could get his time). Our conversation wandered to the importance of training new hires out of college. I went on a rampage about my company's young leaders program. They got senior leaders to give them talks and even threw them quarterly parties. But they were turning them into mindless corporate robots. They sounded like a cliché when they talked, because they were just trying to copy the bosses and their language of trends and discussion points – when we all knew they were kids that knew nothing about it yet. The CEO replied that his daughter was in the program that I had just torn apart. Rather than getting defensive, he simply asked what advice I would give his daughter. I started to answer in corporate jargon, but caught myself and just said: "Tell her to raise the blinds and turn the lights ON when she enters any meeting or conference room".

Listening & Attention

The most important behavior we can exhibit and the most fundamental pattern we can set is to listen, to truly listen. In those strange meetings going on right now in conference rooms around the world, wasting the time of millions of people, they aren't actually listening to one another. They nod their heads and thank each other, but they are not listening; they are not trying on each others' ideas for size; they are not even really present.

When people are busy not listening to each other, they tend to be doing one of two things. Either they are thinking about completely unrelated issues – the shopping, next week's report, sex, whatever – or, in those cases where their attention is in the room, they are usually planning what to say when it's their turn. In fact, one of my favorite quotes from a colleague is: "Listening is not waiting to speak."

So we set an example and create a pattern by truly listening to what is going on. We show we are listening by offering eye contact, by nodding, and occasionally by writing or re-phrasing what we hear. We create a 'listening pattern' by referring to a comment that a participant made earlier, or by flagging when one participant contradicts what another participant said in a different conversation.

I don't know that setting this pattern of listening will influence the ability and willingness of others to listen, but I am confident that if I fail to listen attentively, the participants won't bother even to pretend. The only way I know to set a listening pattern is to pay attention.

One of my biggest facilitation mistakes was an attempt to prove the importance of listening and attention. In an 80-person event in a renovated train station, I kicked off the session by staying totally silent. I maintained total silence until each and every person was staring at me with their whole body. I stayed quiet just a little longer then announced the exact time and asked everyone to look at their watches and acknowledge that this was the first time in the company's history that 80 people were fully concentrated with all their minds on one of their colleagues without a single bit of multi-tasking of any sort going on. I then proceeded to begin the event.

But I had already gone too far. The point was driven so hard that everyone instantly began to wonder and analyze what had just happened. One of my mentors was on the team and asked if I realized what I had done. The team helped me recover in the following modules and the event was a success, but it was the best lesson I could ever have taught myself about facilitating, listening and how to use and abuse our participants' attention.

Attention is such a rare commodity and so many elements in our lives are designed precisely to rob us of it – chimes and bleeps, calls and tweets – that maintaining a small reserve of attention to enable us to truly listen can sometimes feel superhuman. And the only way to maintain that level of attention needed to create constructive, collaborative patterns is to care. I know of no other way.

Servant Leadership

In 1970, Robert Greenleaf coined the term *Servant Leadership*, though the concept is timeless. The name is self-explanatory. Apart from listening, the facilitator must set a pattern of serving. Obviously, the facilitator is at the service of the participants and serving effectively requires both humility and genuine leadership.

More importantly, in a collaborative space, everyone is there to serve everyone else. So when I circulate among the participants during their working lunch, I quietly take away their dishes and cups and tidy their workspace. I do this because I want to facilitate their work and so I remove barriers (dishes) to their work. But I also do it to set a pattern of servant leadership; as a facilitator, I am in a sense a leader, and as a facilitator, I am in a sense a servant. The same holds true for each and every participant and when I set a pattern of servant leadership, my objective is that other participants begin to challenge their expectations of serving and leading and adopt some of this philosophy, or at a minimum, some more collaborative behaviors.

MUSIC

After weeks of fishing for an appointment, a colleague and I finally managed to swing an invitation from Duke University Hospital System to discuss a possible event. We were given a three-hour slot with the vice chancellor and heads of several departments to pitch our services to design and facilitate a conference for the top 120 staff from across the organization to rebuild the way the health system shuffled patients through their care (care management). This was our one chance to make an impression and winning the work might open countless doors in the same organization.

We wanted them to express themselves individually and to ensure that the boss didn't overly influence the ideas of her colleagues, so we came prepared with a Take-a-Panel exercise[14]. But the meeting was at the hospital headquarters and we had neither panels nor flip charts nor any way to make the space *ours*. So we brought cardboard boxes on which they would individually work through the exercise. We got to the meeting room a bit early and prepared our boxes.

---

14   See p. 25

When the meeting began, we did quick introductions and jumped right into the exercise; no presentation about our capabilities and approach, and no chance for the vice chancellor to dictate her expectations and thus shut down further discussion around objectives and outcomes. Of course, they were taken aback at our pushiness and insistence that they do this exercise before discussing the event.

After an awkward minute or two while our presumptuousness sank in, they took their assignment and their boxes and their colored markers and began to work.

And then we switched on the music. They looked up and then looked at each other and then looked at us. We had brought a Bose Bluetooth speaker that they had not noticed. Out of it came *Solo Piano* by Chilly Gonzales[15] at a moderate volume to accompany their work. I suspect that no guests had ever come into their offices, taken over as we had, and then played music.

At first they were surprised, but within a few seconds, they were back to their work; within two minutes it became just another element in the environment that we had created; within five minutes, the music had become necessary. The rhythm of their work, their focus on the task at hand, their ability to ignore each other and interact with their boxes were all dependent on the music. In a few

---

15   http://bkle.in/1Q3omQM

minutes the use of music went from being a bizarre intrusion to being a key element of our work together.

Music *is* a key element of our work. Music facilitates transitions (shifting participants from one mode of work or one place to another) and provides background or wallpaper for small team work. I rely on music as much as I rely on lighting or chairs or a surface to write on. I suppose I could facilitate an event without these elements, but why would I ever want to?

Music for Transitions

I think of music as a bridge spanning a chasm that separates one activity from another. When it's time to call participants to plenary, either to start an event or to herd them at the end of break-out sessions, an *In* song is the signal that something important is about to happen. Then, when it is time to move from plenary into teams, an *Out* song will help them on their way. Other transitions – shifting from team to team or signing up for an activity – are facilitated by other songs.

In

With the right music, we can create a real beginning; a dividing point between whatever was happening before and what we have in store *right now*. If the music is loud enough, it interferes with small talk and signals that something big is about to happen. It sets the tone and the energy for the work at hand.

During an event at the suburban campus of Sprint, a phone company in the Fortune 100, the participants were given a task to build the tallest freestanding marshmallow and spaghetti tower that they could. In no time, competing teams had erected simple structures. And during the 20 minutes or so that they built their towers, my colleagues and I set the chairs for a circular plenary.

How to signal that they should stop building and come take a seat in the plenary area? The energy was high but we needed to pump it higher. Had we simply taken a microphone and asked people to come take a seat, that energy would have dissipated in a matter of seconds.

Instead, we put on U2's *Where the Streets Have No Name*[16]; actually a re-mix with an extended build-up at the beginning. With 50 people focused on their building task and all talking to each other, the noise level was at a sustained roar, like the cabin of a jetliner during takeoff. So we started the song loud and then made it louder so that by the one-minute mark, when the guitar and drums come in, the song filled the enormous room. By the time the words kicked in (1:46), conversation was impossible and the participants knew, without being told, that it was time to gather together to launch our work.

By the time the song ended, all 50 participants were seated, focused, and primed for a potentially career-changing three days. The song was scaled to the participants, the room, and the work we were setting off to tackle together. Big challenge, big song.

At a 60-person event for an outsourcing call center the following week, using such a powerful song to kick-off a lower-key two-day event would have seemed absurd. The energy was out of scale to our facilitation task. I kicked the event off with the Afro-Cuban All-Stars' *Distinto, Diferente*[17], an energetic song, but more in scale with the event we were facilitating.

A week later, at a much smaller event for a tight group of executives addressing fraud, waste and abuse, I kicked off with Neil Young's *Tell Me Why*[18], a much lower-energy, more pensive song. In this case, the participants, who all knew each other from previous events, were busy greeting each other and my need was to create a more thoughtful, challenging environment. The song served to bridge the energy level I found in the room with the one I needed to create in order to launch their work.

*I make the same considerations when choosing an In song to bring partici-*pants back to plenary at the end of small group work. What is their

---

16   http://bkle.in/1TyQhxU

17   http://bkle.in/1QaewAj

18   http://bkle.in/1LB9BmC

current energy level? What level of energy do I need to make the plenary session work? Can I find a song that will serve to carry the participants from where they are to where I want them to be?

As the day proceeds, participants often need an energy boost – and a song that they are familiar with, something with just the right beat, serves to re-charge them. You can tell: they come back to plenary practically dancing to the music. I often serve candy at this time as well, but I'm pretty sure it is the music that makes the difference.

Covers and re-mixes often have special power to affect participants; they create something new out of the familiar, which is what the event as a whole is so often trying to achieve. The Neptunes re-mix of the Rolling Stones' *Sympathy for the Devil*[19] provides a wonderful example. This is a re-mix with a light touch. It adds very few new riffs and it takes away some of what we're accustomed to: trading acoustic for electric guitar in the "Just as every cop is a criminal..." phrase; the four-beat pause before "Pleased to meet you..." And perhaps because the re-mix is so subtle, it helps us hear the original as if for the first time.

Whatever the song, an *In* says: "Stop what you're doing! Come together!" It signals a new beginning.

Out

Choosing the right song to accompany participants from a plenary session to their break-outs – an *Out* – is more critical than an *In* because the stakes are higher. An *In* which fails to set the right energy level is more a lost opportunity than a problem. On the other hand, the wrong *Out* can have an immediate cost to the effectiveness of the group. The *Out* sets up a team for their next, largely-unsupervised task and plays a key role in determining how they approach that task.

Without music, a facilitator signals that a team activity is about to begin and invites participants to move to their new team areas. As they shuffle out of plenary, a deathly silence descends on the room and whatever energy or sense of anticipation or healthy impatience simply vanishes. Participants make their way to their break-out, look

---

19   http://bkle.in/1Q3nxaW

at each other slightly embarrassed, and awkwardly try to remember what they were asked to do. It might take 10 or 15 minutes to recreate the focus and energy that the facilitator applied her skills to create.

The right song at the right moment can all but eliminate that collapse in focus and energy; it serves as a bridge to transport participants from their mental state in plenary to their collaborative mode of working in break-outs.

How to choose that song? A bridge needs to be anchored at both ends. So the song needs to grow from the plenary session that is ending, in spirit, in energy, and perhaps even with its lyrics. It then needs to set the right tone for the break-out work that is about to begin. Ideally, the plenary session seamlessly sets up the subsequent break-out sessions, so the energy level at the close of plenary is the desired level for the break-outs. The song serves as an energy bridge; its vibe bounds from the plenary discussion and its beat carries the participants to their next task.

To bridge the awkward silence that otherwise follows a plenary session, it must be a song with a pronounced beat at the beginning; a song that fades in gradually won't work. And that initial beat should be in time with the facilitator's closing words: "Let's get to work!" ... boom! (the first beat of the song). It may seem like an insanely precise way to time the start of a song, but when it is in perfect tempo with the facilitator's words, the purpose of the song as a bridge across which participants travel suddenly makes sense.

Up, Shift, Sign-up

Other sorts of transitions benefit from other types of music. We often play a warning song – an *Up*, just prior to the *In* to signal to break-out groups that their time is running out. I will choose an instrumental song that slowly builds in energy. For example, in a more intimate event, if I am using classical music, I might play the two-minute march from Beethoven's *Fidelio*[20]. For a larger event, I might choose something more energetic and longer, like Nina

---

[20]   http://bkle.in/1SKVFxV

Simone's Sinnerman[21], which communicates urgency and impatience. I will start at a low volume that participants might not notice as they are immersed in their team activities. I will gradually raise the volume over the nine minutes of the song until by the last few minutes it is quite loud and participants have to nearly shout to be heard above the din.

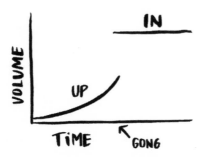

As intrusive as the Up song is, participants seem to take the growing energy in their stride; as the song becomes louder and more insistent, their work becomes more frantic as they wrap up and prepare for the plenary session that is about to start. (But I hate it when restaurants try the same trick to turn tables faster).

Other transitions also call for musical support. A song to shift people between teams mustn't be as energetic as an In because we don't want them to return to plenary, but it must certainly signal a change. I will start this sort of Shift song gradually, so participants know they must wrap up their current discussion and move on, without it being so loud that they can't finish their thoughts.

At other times, we want participants to get out of their chairs quickly and sign up to a task or a team or a role. We're in a hurry and we want them to feel our urgency, so we choose a Sign-up song that mirrors this frenetic task.

Whatever the transition we are planning, choosing an appropriate song will make that transition more effective. Music moves us all so we use music to move our participants.

Wallpaper Music

Work in small teams also benefits from music. This light background music – wallpaper – serves to camouflage the voices in adjoining teams, thereby allowing break-outs to work close together with less interference.

More importantly, wallpaper enables the facilitator to regulate the energy level of the teams at work. Wallpaper music lends the facilitator remarkable power. If I feel that participants in break-outs are working too fast and risk being too superficial, I merely have to shift to lower-energy, perhaps minor-key music and the energy and focus of the teams will adjust within a minute or two. Participants are rarely aware of this tool and their ignorance makes the tool that much more powerful.

When choosing wallpaper, I avoid music with lyrics. First, I don't want to worry about subliminal meaning that might enter the team conversations. Second, I don't want participants to raise their voices in order to compete with a voice coming over the loudspeakers. In fact, I even avoid instruments – saxophone, clarinet – that sound vaguely like the human voice, in order to minimize the interference in their conversations.

I tend to use jazz or, occasionally, classical music. I also pay close attention to the age and preferences of the participants (especially if I can get data beforehand). For groups under 45 years old, which is admittedly not as often as I prefer, I switch to modern/pop music intermittently, but not enough so that it feels like they are on a bus or hanging out with their kids. If people are working individually, I may choose a piano solo; if in pairs, I may choose a duet. I tend to keep the volume very low, though as an event proceeds, I find myself raising it bit by bit as the teams' ability to self-regulate the noise level improves. By the end of an event, the music can be surprisingly loud, which matches the increasing intensity of the work.

Taking the role of music further, we gave groups of three from the earlier-mentioned Global Shapers session an assignment to create an instrument with their voices. We knew of a young musician in the group of 60 participants and asked her to lead (conduct) the experiment and the groups. We started with just one group at a time using their 'instruments' and then we had them retell the story of the graphic facilitation white board that visually captured the morning's discussions. I can't say it sounded great, but those voice instruments showed up continuously for the next day and a half, adding an energy to the group that I have rarely seen since.

Energy is so important that frequently during the final hours of the participants' time with me, I'll increase the beat of my songs and gradually build the entire room towards higher-quality output as the music crescendos.

Just Music

Facilitating without music is unthinkable for me. But what about facilitating *only* with music? So far it is just a thought experiment, but I do occasionally consider how to design and facilitate an event in which my only tool for interacting with participants – for guiding their work, helping them find their way, shaping the energy in the room, finding new levels of recursion to provide new vantage points – is the music I choose to play.

So my only tools would be rhythm, tempo, key, melody, harmony, and volume. I would provide no spoken instructions and I would be out-of-sight. Could the music facilitate on its own? Perhaps one day I'll let the experiment out of the lab of my imagination.

DIFFICULT PARTICIPANTS

Difficult participants fall into two categories: snipers and terrorists. Snipers have an enemy in their sights that they are waiting to pick off. The enemy might be another participant – say a rival, or the boss – or it might be a particular policy or product or potential outcome. Their rifle is always loaded and if the intended target isn't an easy shot, the facilitator can always stand in as a proxy.

Terrorists are after the whole group and the entire event. In their view, this event should never have happened and the questions being asked should never have been broached. They want to take everyone out and are happy to sacrifice themselves to the cause. Like Lord

Salisbury, British Prime Minister at the turn of the 20th Century, they believe that "whatever happens will be for the worse, and therefore it is in our interests that as little should happen as possible."

When confronted with one of these undesirables, it is important to remember that we are not part of the system that they are attacking. They may turn their fire on us, but we are, at most, symbols of their true target and often no more than innocent bystanders. Yet as facilitators, it is our task to disarm these difficult participants.

I have a few strategies I employ when faced with these characters. These strategies tend to work better with snipers than with terrorists, perhaps because snipers are often satisfied so long as they have a single victim, even if that victim is me. Terrorists, on the other hand, won't rest until the event is perceived as a failure.

The easiest to deal with are those who have beliefs contrary to those of their colleagues. They either have a different set of facts from the other participants or they use the same facts but arrive at different conclusions. My strategy? I give them the benefit of the doubt; I imagine that they might be right. Often they are.

When these people become aggressive, it is usually because they don't feel listened to. So I listen. I genuinely listen and treat their comments with the same dignity as anyone else's. Perhaps I write them down for all to see. Which is to say, I treat both them and their ideas with respect.

Somewhat more difficult are those who condescend to me because, since I am an outsider, they can; and in so doing they assert their status or, through me, attack a colleague whom I am believed to speak for. These cases require much more humility. My strategy is to absorb it, while reminding myself that the attack isn't really meant for me. I acknowledge what was said and I don't push back.

These bullies can be most effective when they frame their attacks as questions. "So how do you plan to reconcile these views?" they ask, knowing full well that I do not know how to reconcile these views and that they might be irreconcilable. "Why don't *you* tell us how to deliver the care management programs on time?", I was challenged by a senior healthcare provider once.

As much as I may be tempted to, I *never* answer these questions.

Doing so would be like accepting a dare. I tend to adopt a two-step response. First, I turn the question back to the whole room: "How *will* we reconcile these views?" I ask. "Does anyone here know how to deliver these care management programs on time and want to share the secret with the rest of us?"

Then I try to escape to a higher order: "If we fail to reconcile these views," I ask, what do we lose as a team? Can we move forward without reconciling them?" To the healthcare group: "What products *do* we deliver on time? What can we learn from these successes?"

I step out of the way of the aggressive question and try to build it into the flow of the discussion, as if the bully were doing me a favor. I triangulate; I turn an opposition into a mere data point; a potentially-valuable data point.

Harder still is when participants interrupt a discussion to tell me how I should be facilitating or how the event should have been designed or what we should be doing next. These people are often consultants or ex-consultants and they know just enough about facilitation to be really disruptive. In these cases, I stand on firmer ground since, unlike challenges on facts or conclusions, the facilitation process really is mine and I will defend it. I still try to avoid direct confrontation, but after entertaining the possibility that the challenger might be right (and incorporating her approach in case she is right), I will forcefully describe – not explain – the next step of the process. I never ask participants to engage in a particular exercise; I tell them. So when I am challenged on process, the same forcefulness doesn't come across as defensive. The unspoken message is: you participants look after the event's content and I will support you; I, the facilitator, will look after the process and I expect you to support me.

I apply these strategies to both snipers and terrorists. Where my strategies differ concerns integration or isolation: I work to integrate the snipers and to isolate the terrorists. I make a special effort to ensure that the snipers are not seated at the edge of the plenary. I make sure they are in particularly dynamic break-outs with the smartest and most articulate participants. If they hog the limelight in plenary, I will walk over and stand uncomfortably close, which can seem aggressive and it is; but it heightens their connection to me and the group.

With terrorists, on the other hand, I discourage contact. They tend to sit away from the other participants and I don't interfere. If, in plenary, they attack the premise of the event itself or work to undermine the shared intent that is emerging among the other participants, I will turn my back and make eye contact with as many other participants as possible. There are moments when their skepticism can be constructive and in those moments, I will use my own words to convey the terrorist's issues, but I will try to avoid calling on him.

Break-outs are more delicate as I can't always supervise and intervene. Sometimes I adopt the Edward Teller approach. During the Manhattan Project, a US-led initiative which developed nuclear weapons in the 1940s, one physicist, Edward Teller, did not collaborate well with the other lead scientists, particularly Hans Bethe and Robert Oppenheimer, head of the Los Alamos lab. Despite his evident brilliance as a physicist, he was disrupting the enormously creative work of the other scientists and putting the project at risk. Rather than exclude him from the project, he was partially sidelined by being given related projects (theorizing the H-bomb and studying the risk that the atomic bomb might ignite the atmosphere) that he could conduct with minimal interaction with the principal work at Los Alamos.[22]

When I have a participant who risks blowing up the entire event – a terrorist – I try to find a potentially useful but isolated task for him to do and politely keep him away from the 'real' work going on elsewhere.

I find that *every* event has its difficult participants and in most cases they need to be taken very seriously. They are rarely the loners they appear to be. Usually other participants harbor the same doubts or the same wish to see a colleague undermined or the event unravel. The fact that one participant has stepped forward to play the sniper

---

22   After the war, Teller got his revenge both by raising doubts about Oppenheimer's loyalty, which cost the latter his security clearance, and by leading the H-Bomb project.

or the terrorist merely relieves the others of the need to do so themselves. Yet I have never found myself in an event when I didn't feel that the vast majority of participants were on my side, wanting desperately for me to succeed because, in doing so, they would succeed as well.

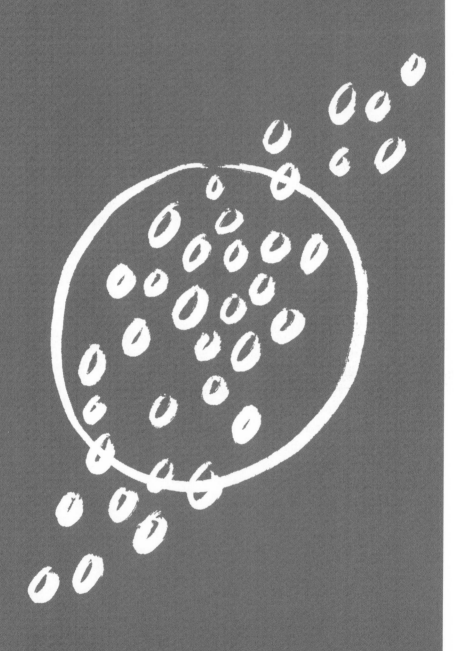

CHAPTER 8
VALUE CAPTURE

Unlike consultants, whose engagements tend to last for many months or even years, facilitators have much smaller canvases to work on. The lifecycle of our events rarely extends beyond three or four months, while the event itself can last from a few hours to at most three or four days. During that brief period, we get so caught up in the moment that we can lose sight of what happens afterwards, when the potential value we help create is either realized or not.

Participants usually leave our events on a high. They feel as if they have seen the invisible and achieved the impossible. Yet they have done nothing of the sort. At best, our work has created the *potential* for change. The value of our work evaporates in hours or at most days after the event unless we, our sponsors, and the event participants make a conscious effort to channel that potential and capture the value that our clients are paying for.

The odds against effective value capture are very long. Participants have been out of the office for the duration of the event and on their return are faced with an overwhelming backlog of emails, calls, meetings, and other distractions from the plans that were agreed to at the end of the event. Even worse, every office behavior, every business process, and every management hierarchy exists to eliminate variation and stifle change. The best of intentions at the end of a successful event are no match for the inertia that our participants face on Monday morning, standing by the coffee machine, logging back into the server and reading the latest policy to descend from heaven.

I believe that we can build much of the needed value capture into our event designs. We design agendas and individual modules to help participants step up to being change leaders, to help them identify barriers and how to overcome them; we guide them through the detailed design of timelines, GANTTs, RACIs, transformation maps, job descriptions, commitment statements, budgets, ambitious strategies, and detailed action plans. This is the job of an event designer.

But design is largely outside the scope of this book. Here we are looking at the behaviors that facilitators employ to bring those designs to life and shape the energy of participants. In that narrow role, what can facilitators do during an event to increase the likelihood of value capture in the weeks and months that follow?

Signal vs. Noise

I believe that the single most important role a facilitator can play to ensure value capture is to stay focused on the difference between signal and noise; between the ideas and insights that could have potential long-term value and other observations that cloud the vision of those charged with implementing the event's outcomes.

Let's be honest: our events create a lot of noise. Our job is not to find the shortest path from A to B but to open up a world of possibilities and help the people we're facilitating to converge on a very small number of those possibilities. We then help them dissect the surviving ideas and draft them into road maps that might sketch out the way towards creating value. That journey is full of dead ends and blind alleys. A lot of great ideas have to fall away in order to reveal the even better idea that is worth pursuing once the event is over. As the noise gets louder and louder, we help the participants identify the *signal* – the gem of potential value – that lies within.

Following an event in 2009 for Cisco, the networking giant, we created the noise that video was going to be a big deal online. Cisco took it so seriously that they bought webcams for the entire division. However, even the networking giant itself wasn't prepared for video bandwidth at every desk. So the webcams got tossed onto tables in the middle of the cubicles as a reminder of the 'noise.'

However, this wasn't for nothing, as it opened almost all employees' minds to the potential of video. They proceeded to buy Flip Video, the small action cameras that recorded to a flash drive that were all the rage at the time (until mobile phone video became more convenient and Cisco closed down the division in 2011). Not to lose heart though, Cisco have succeeded massively with Telepresence and WebEx where millions of people continue to exchange video together. Cisco got the signal of video for the long run, but acted on the noise far too rapidly on multiple occasions.

We are outside the system that we are facilitating. This distance offers us a distinct advantage in distinguishing the signal from the noise. Our participants are usually inside the system and thus often fail to challenge or even identify the assumptions that underpin the functioning of that system.

Fortunately, the very skill that we facilitators employ to shape a conversation – amplifying constructive signals and attenuating destructive signals – is the same skill that increases the chance of value capture. As these constructive signals begin to stand out from the noise, our job is to provide new perspective and new language so that participants can make use of them. When we help participants find a novel way to describe an insight, that new description is likely to make its way back to the day-to-day. In fact, it is *only* when an image or a metaphor or a neologism or a story becomes associated with a constructive signal that this signal has a hope of standing out from the noise.

In our event creating the first Accountable Care Organization in Tucson mentioned earlier, we were searching for strategies that would allow the large local hospital to catalyze a variety of other health providers to serve patients better and keep them healthier, since financial reimbursement would now be tied to health outcomes and not just billing for more and more services. Once these investments were in place and a certain critical mass or self-sustaining level of activity had been achieved, the hospital would see the right patients and not Emergency Room visits for urgent care needs or virtual visits for even simpler remedies. Had we discussed this strategy as being a 'catalyst', though accurate, it would not have fixed this concept in the minds of the participants. Instead, we introduced the metaphor of role-playing skits to capture the nature of their intention to catalyze and then step back. We literally had each small group of leaders act out with costumes and props how this would all come together. Each team created a metaphor for how the health system should work. I wish I still had the video of these now famous healthcare leaders dressed up and acting out the reinvention of healthcare in Tucson.

The vivid image of a fully-animated participant skit helped the participants and especially the sponsors to focus on this two-step approach – build and withdraw – in a way that shaped the resulting strategy. That the metaphor 'stuck' helped us all understand that this was a signal and not noise.

This ability to use language to distinguish between signal and noise during an event becomes even more important once the event is over. Thus the facilitator's role to increase the chances of effective value capture is in detecting these signals and giving them the linguistic power to survive the onslaught of noise that awaits them once the event is over.

Follow-up

The days immediately following our events are critical to ensure that they represent a true inflection point rather than an interruption. For an event to leave a mark, the most urgent task is to get the participant's work back to them in a form that they can use to explain to others (and thus to themselves) what it is that was actually achieved.

Many Executive Summaries capture event highlights without distinguishing between signal and noise. A more useful document builds on a very few themes (the signal) and ignores, as much as possible, the rest. In the period immediately following the event – ideally the same evening – we tend to involve sponsors in a detailed discussion to identify those few insights and those high-impact actions that will have a lasting effect on the organization. Wherever possible, we try to use the participants' own words and perhaps even their hand-written work, to help keep alive the memory of what is important and what isn't. When a metaphor helped to make a signal stand out – say ecosystems or skits – we will make use of that metaphor with words and illustrations in our summary document.

In the weeks that follow, I try to use that Executive Summary as a starting point for team discussions with the client. In the best of circumstances, we keep the sponsor team alive after the event and shift its role from event ownership and co-design to program management, but building on the same collaborative habits we developed during the planning phase for the event.

We held an event for Optum, a $70 billion subsidiary of UnitedHealth Group, to align its strategy with that of the Mayo Clinic to create a collaborative research and innovation center to solve the greatest challenges in healthcare – including the sharing of tens of millions of clinical and insurance records (de-identified of course) to make this possible. Prior to the session, a large number of executives produced a very detailed transition plan, outlining milestones, responsibilities, resources, and KPIs; just the sort of detail that, when produced by a consultant, sits on the shelf and collects dust. We wanted to show that since the employees most affected by this change were the authors of this change plan, they would be much more likely to actually implement it. To improve the chances of making these actions come to life, we did three things:

1. During the beginning of the session, I brushed up against the 4ft x 6ft foam board detailing the objectives and toppled it onto the Mayo Clinic CEO's head. Although every Optum leader nearly had a heart attack, the CEO smiled, gave me a little pat on the back and went right to work. This 'topple' eased the tension in the room, opened everyone up to the design format and set the tone for 'collaboration no matter what happens'.

2. Our preparation team took every single Optum product and service offering, and rewrote its description into the Mayo clinic language. Then they aligned it to Mayo's strategy on a 50-foot wide version of their operating model.

3. We held a brief planning session at the very end of our event in which all participants nominated project managers from within the work teams while the sponsor team committed publicly to meet fortnightly to oversee the transition.

Four years later, several of the sponsor team are still together and, best of all, they continue to use the sort of collaborative methods and tools that had made them so effective during our design work together. We held these meetings in their offices, playing their game, but with more and more of our rules thrown into the mix. I facilitated these sessions frequently but increasingly a leader who seemed to understand our approach would step up and take on this task.

Needless to say, the transition plan was implemented on schedule and the expected results were exceeded. The value that was created during the event itself needed that on-going light-touch facilitation to allow it to take root. I am proud that the Optum-Mayo Clinic partnership has now made breakthroughs and the head of public policy for AARP says, "The quality and the usefulness of the research will not only change clinical practice but also help change patients' understanding of their care..." – when it all could have been destroyed because I accidentally hit the CEO.

In this case, the event content needed a helping hand from us in order to survive the inevitable deadening effect of business-as-usual. On other cases, the facilitation environment itself and the collaborative behaviors it engenders need to be grafted onto the client's way of working.

The Obamacare response events mentioned earlier had developed deeply-engrained ways of working which, while not un-collaborative, were so siloed that crippling complexity had crept into any design or business decision that needed to be made. During our event, multiple sub-projects emerged, each with its own sponsor team. The post-event risk was that these projects would themselves succumb to the complexity that they were designed to cut through. So my colleagues installed a permanent facilitation environment in the client's headquarters. This space resembled the large environment that we had prepared for our initial event, but much smaller and sited near the lead sponsor's office. Indeed, the collaboration/facilitation space was so prevalent at the headquarters, that the room had no walls on two sides, so our music would fill the air of the 1,500 people with desks in the office. It slowly became the place to solve the day-to-day problems that arose during the implementation of these sub-projects; a sort of un-tangling environment.

In both these examples, the event served to isolate the signal from the noise. In the case of the Mayo Clinic, the signal consisted of content – projects to align complex processes and integrate data for the benefit of all. In the case of Obamacare, the signal was more conceptual; it was the ability and desire to recognize the latent simplicity that lies at the heart of many overly- and overtly-complex business cultures. Having identified those signals, our task during and, above all, after our events, was to find a way to accompany that signal as it gradually settled into our clients' ways of working.

CHAPTER 9
SATISFACTION

Workshops and conferences frequently end with a short satisfaction survey being circulated among the participants. I rarely use these surveys since I am more concerned with whether the sponsors believe they achieved their objectives than whether participants had a good time. Usually, participants have a wonderful time, which skews any satisfaction survey towards 'Outstanding', thus rendering the survey less than objective and dispassionate.

Did the sponsors achieve their objectives? It is usually too soon to say; we might not know for months. It is relatively easy to check whether we produced the desired outcomes, but the real value of those outcomes can only be judged in hindsight and only when their contribution to the event's objectives and its deeper purpose can be assessed.

What about *my* satisfaction and that of my team? When I look back on an event, what gives me a sense of satisfaction and achievement? There are a few attributes that are shared by many of the events that I found most satisfying to facilitate.

Of course, I enjoy those events that are challenging, in which seemingly-impossible outcomes were achieved. I enjoy big events, with lots of complexity and which permit me to work with a big enough team of colleagues. My favorite events had fifty to eighty participants and a team of at least seven.

I enjoy events in wonderful venues. I once facilitated an event in the Atlanta Aquarium, at one point the largest in the world. The beluga whales were mating and after participants witnessed that for three days, the complexity of the business objectives was downright simple. I've worked in palaces, the tops of New York skyscrapers, and my personal favorite... having break-out groups on a private section of the Great Wall of China. After a short hike and then sitting on the ancient work of thousands, overlooking increasingly smog-filled rolling hills, it's impossible not to contemplate all the ramifications of every decision. How can that not be satisfying? My only mandate when I got married however, was that it wasn't in a hotel ballroom.

Events which stretched our team and relied on their judgment leave me feeling satisfied. In an event for a large car insurance company, our team felt that the real issue was the way the company was structured and that the participants would never open that up as part of the conversation. So when the participants returned on the second morning, our entire team of 10, including four graphic artists, re-created the company based on the Hollywood studio model. The visuals were so effective that the session was responsible for restructuring the organization into a more effective, agile, Hollywood-style network of experts to deliver the insurance solutions needed. We gave them the language to create a new company without angering anyone. They felt liberated by our presumptuousness and tackled issues that had remained unaddressed for many years.

ROUNDNESS

One attribute shared by all of the most satisfying events is *roundness*. I often describe the arc of an event; how it develops a narrative and passes through moments of doubt or crisis and then lands firmly in a safe and desired place. Achieving this narrative arc is more a function of design than of facilitation.

Once in a while, though, the arc closes in on itself and becomes a circle. In the most satisfying events of all, we discover that our point of arrival is precisely our point of departure, but that it, and we, are changed somehow. Like an astronaut flying into space and returning to her launch pad, she is back where she started, but the launch pad is somehow different. It, and she, are new.

Roundness is the quality of completeness, of returning to our starting point and discovering that it is new, of discovering that we knew the answer all along, only now we *believe* it and we discover that it is both familiar and unexpected at the same time.

It is paradoxical that the most satisfying events are those which transport us not to somewhere new but to the very place we started. Those journeys which take us someplace new and then bring us back home are often the most dangerous – just ask Ulysses or Dorothy or Bilbo Baggins. But thanks to how our journey has transformed us, the home we return to is entirely new.

Brandon Klein is a facilitator and designer of collaborative processes with a focus on artificial intelligence. He is currently a partner at the Difference Consulting and is a member of the Value Web. He lives in Minneapolis.

Dan Newman is a facilitator and designer of collaborative processes. He is a partner in Matter Group and is a member of the Value Web. He lives in Rome and London.

58268507R00100

Made in the USA
Columbia, SC
18 May 2019